Conversation Tactics

43 Verbal Strategies to Charm, Captivate, Banter, and Defend

By Patrick King
Social Interaction Specialist and
Conversation Coach
www.PatrickKingConsulting.com

Table of Contents

Conversation Tactics 43 Verbal Strategies to Charm, Captivate, Banter, and Defend 3

Table of Contents 5

Foreword by Steve Scott 7

Introduction 11

Chapter 1. Pre-Conversation 17
   Warming Up Psychologically 18
   Warming Up Physically 24
   The Conversation Résumé 31
   Fallback Stories 36

Chapter 2. Setting the Tone 47
   Speak Like Friends 49
   Find Similarity 53
   Strategically Swear 62
   Get People Talking 66

Chapter 3. How to Be Captivating 71
   Life Is a Series of Stories 72
   The 1:1:1 Method 78
   Ask for Stories 82
   Use Stories to Create Inside Jokes 90

Chapter 4. Charm Offensive 95
   Compliments 96
   Listening with Intent 102
   Turn Enemies into Friends 108
   Interrupting to Agree 114

Chapter 5. Slipping Away and Out 121

The Psychology of Leaving 122
The Great Escape 130

Chapter 6. Specific [Awkward] Situations . 139
What's Your Name, Again? 142
Accepting Compliments 146
Breaking the Ice 151
Dealing with Interruptions 156

Chapter 7. Stop, Please 163
You Only See Black and White 166
You Give Unsolicited Thoughts 170
You Are Creepy 173
You Always Laugh First 177

Chapter 8. Self-Defense 185
How to Say No 186
How to Deflect and Roll with the Punches 195
Always Admit Wrong 205
Dealing with Passive-Aggressiveness 208

Chapter 9. On the Offensive 217
Best Practices 218
No Ad Hominem 227
Appeal to Perfection 231
Sowing Seeds of Doubt 234
Clarifying Questions 238
Beat the Strawman 241

Conclusion 247

Speaking and Coaching 251

Cheat Sheet 253

Foreword by Steve Scott

My name is Steve Scott and I'm a *Wall Street Journal* bestselling author. I'm also known as *The Habits Guy* on occasion. I've known Patrick for a while and it's not just because we've bonded over the incredible geekiness of visiting Hobbiton in New Zealand (someday…) or have a mutual love for running absurdly long distances.

We became fast friends after a few chance emails and I was taken by how warm and inquisitive he was about me. We had just met and it felt like we had known each other for years. *How did he do that?*

I purchased one of his books out of curiosity and quickly found out. For those that are unaware, Patrick has coached social skills and communication skills for years and writes on the same topic. I found out that his coaching practice was no joke, and he really knew what he was talking about because I read about techniques to build rapport that he had used on me—with great success. *Conversation Tactics* is a book that boils down many of these similar aspects into bite-sized golden nuggets. If you're seeking advice on how to talk to anyone and navigate social situations, you'll find it here.

I recall Patrick once told me about a client that was struggling with holding conversations with women he was interested in. At the end of their time together, he reported being able to hold conversations with just about anyone and had tied down his first girlfriend in eight years. The proof is in the pudding.

This isn't your normal book on keeping eye contact or the oft-repeated tip of boiling small talk down to *FORD—family, occupation, recreation, and dreams*. This is an analytical dissection of conversation from someone who has broken it down with fervor. It's a collection of knowledge that just might win you a new friend or save an old relationship.

Patrick has my full endorsement, not because we're friends but because he lives what he preaches.

—*Steve Scott, Author of the bestselling book Habit Stacking and head honcho at www.developgoodhabits.com*

Introduction

Just like Republicans have Democrats, vampires have the sun, and cats have everything under the sun, I have natural enemies. We all do.

In life, there are simply people who push your buttons and whose feathers you ruffle. Some people like baseball and hate soccer, and to some people you are soccer. There's no rhyme or reason, just a gut negative feeling.

But I digress. My arch nemesis when I was growing up was named *Kyle*. We all have a *Kyle*.

Kyle was the proverbial thorn in my side. It seemed like everything I said annoyed him on a personal level, which would then cause him to loudly disagree. He would express himself to anyone that would listen about how wrong I was and expound on everything that I didn't know. Unfortunately, we shared the same group of friends so we were forced into interaction constantly. Since I continued to offend him by breathing and existing, we would bicker like a married couple.

One of our biggest arguments was about choosing where to eat after a group canoeing trip. We clashed as usual, but this time he used some dirty argument tactics that I didn't know how to counter. He was somehow able to label me as selfish and uncaring to the needs of the group. Needless to say, I was stumped and lost that argument and we went to his restaurant of choice.

To this day, I can't be sure if he actually felt maliciously toward me, but I just couldn't win with him. Over the years, I learned to deal with him and eventually convert him into a friend. As you might guess from the aim of this book, it was a process of using conversation to disarm and befriend my old nemesis Kyle.

The first step was learning how to get him to accept and tolerate me. It was a matter of speaking his language, understanding his perspective, and projecting my respect for him in a tangible way. These are things you might think you're doing, but it requires more than just a bit of awareness and effort.

Next, I needed to befriend him and become more than an acquaintance. Despite our constant run-ins, we really didn't know each other very well. If I could get into his inner circle, I could get that same type of snarky argumentation on my side, and that could be valuable. Making someone feel validated and heard is the carpool lane to deeper friendships, especially when you combine it with humor.

Finally, I learned to defend myself from the extraneous and often off-base accusations and arguments he was making. Along with making sure that I was heard and people didn't take advantage of me, it forced him to respect me more and think twice.

I had figured out how to turn a mortal enemy

into a good friend, though the principles are widely applicable to those you wish to charm, befriend, and defend yourself from. I've turned acquaintances into allies and good friends into best friends. It's not that I have a magnetic superpower—quite the contrary. I was more likely the person in the background studying what people said to each other and how they subsequently reacted. Once you realize that conversation can be formulaic and predictable to a certain degree, it becomes clear on how to talk to others to get the reaction you want.

In this book are techniques and tactics, eminently actionable, to make yourself a more smooth and likable person through conversation. *Just* conversation? The subtleties and nuances are what will set you apart, and that's what you'll learn here. Some of what's in this book is the difference between being in the inner circle and being on the outside looking in.

Perhaps most importantly are the tactics to argue and defend yourself effectively. Not everyone you come across, even on a daily basis, has reason to be nice to you. Therefore, learning to assert yourself and stand your grand is an essential part of conversation tactics. If you've ever felt like you were a doormat, this is where your revolution begins.

I realize the skeptical doubts that conversation tactics are no different than manipulating others and putting on a fake front just to desperately make people like you. They can be used for that, but conversation tactics aren't isolated stunts to get a reaction. They are like the background music in a television scene. When they're there, you don't notice that everything is flowing smoothly. They just do, and friendships just form. But when they're gone, you notice (sometimes immediately) that something is just off, and that alone can kill a conversation.

In any case, welcome to *Conversation Tactics*, where the devil is in the details and there is more than meets the eye.

Chapter 1. Pre-Conversation

Sure, you might be excited about throwing yourself into the midst of a conversation and seeing what you can accomplish. That's what motivation can do to someone, but that would be a mistake for the time being. It would be akin to running into battle without your shield, sword, or even horse.

There's more to conversation than thinking off the cuff and creating witty banter out of nothing at all. Very few of us are capable of doing that on a consistent basis, and what's more sustainable, easy, and practical is preparing for a conversation beforehand. To be specific, you're not preparing for specific conversations like they are job interviews—

rather, you are preparing yourself to be able to shine in conversations in general. There's a distinct difference between the two. When you prepare for conversations, you'll find being witty much more available and easy.

By the way, don't let the metaphor be lost in the scuffle—there are definite ways that a shield, sword, and horse relate to preparing yourself to conversation. You never know when you'll need to defend or deflect something (shield), assert something or change the topic (sword), or jump on your proverbial horse to carry you the heck out of there.

Warming Up Psychologically

The first step to pre-conversation is to get ready psychologically—so you're not caught with your pants down in meeting someone new.

"Don't talk to strangers." As children, most of us got this piece of advice drilled into us countless times by our parents. Indeed, this well-meaning instruction might have served us well in our childhood, when we were likely to be gullible prey to sly criminals. Now, as adults, we seemed to have continued harboring the same habit of choosing not to talk to strangers.

In public places, we stick our ears with headphones and glue our faces to our phones, preferring to keep our interactions with people we don't know to the bare minimum. Is this habit still serving us well? Likely not if your goal is to become better at conversation and charm. At the very least, it leaves us woefully unprepared for engaging with people, exposed as if we were ambushed in the middle of the night.

A study by Epley and Schroeder (2014) divided commuters on trains and buses into three groups—the first was instructed to interact with a stranger near them, the second to keep to themselves, and the third to commute as normal. Even though participants in each group predicted feeling more positive if they only kept to themselves, the outcome of the experiment was the opposite. At the end of their ride, the group of commuters who connected with a stranger reported a more positive experience than those who remained disconnected.

In support of the above findings, another study by Sandstrom and Dunn (2013) revealed how being our usual, efficiency-driven selves while buying our daily cup of coffee is robbing us of an opportunity to be happier. While we routinely rush through the transaction without so much as a smile, the study found that people who smiled and engaged in a brief conversation with the barista experienced more positive feelings than those who stuck to the impersonal, efficient approach.

What do these studies reveal about us? Two main things. One, we tend to think we're better off keeping to ourselves than having short interactions with strangers. Two, we're wrong about number one. The simple act of engaging people in short bursts will make us happier and more social, and it will also get us into the habit of warming up psychologically to conversations no matter the context.

We need to engage in more short interactions—or what Steven Handel calls

"10-second relationships"—with others, because they have the potential to make us happier individuals who experience the world in a positive way. When we engage in genuine connections with people, we lessen our sense of isolation and open ourselves up to new ways of seeing things. We come away not only with our hearts fuller, but also with our eyes capable of new perspectives and our minds more enriched by learning more of the world we live in.

Of course, though we may now recognize the benefits of short interactions, it's still understandable how the thought of striking up a conversation with a total stranger may be uninviting or even repulsive to those of us who aren't social butterflies. We feel ill-equipped to engage in fruitful social interactions, so we prefer the loneliness of keeping to ourselves. How do we counter this and warm ourselves up for routinely interacting with others? How do we get into the habit of being interested in people and build enough social confidence so we can turn that interest into meaningful interactions?

By keeping it short and being consistent. Every day, you encounter multiple opportunities for warming up to interactions and building your social confidence. Grab these opportunities as they arise, and limit yourself to 10 seconds—no more, no less. This keeps the hurdle low and attainable so you can begin to see these everywhere you go.

For instance, think of your typical day. On your way to work, how many people do you spend at least some time ignoring—whether those you pass by on the street, sit with in commute, or stand beside in elevators? Greet at least one of those people with "*Good morning*" and offer either a compliment ("*Nice coat. The fabric looks cozy.*"), an observation ("*The sky's cloudless today. Looks like the showers are letting up.*"), or a question ("*I see you're reading John Grisham. Which of his novels is your favorite?*").

For lunch, do you eat solo, hunched over your work desk? Try instead to spend your lunch hour someplace with shared seating, such as your office pantry or a nearby picnic area. Sit beside a colleague you always see in your building yet never got the chance to talk to, and get the conversation rolling by asking about recent company events ("*I heard your department is starting a new leg of research. How's it going?*").

Finally, as you pick up groceries on your way home, chat with another shopper mulling over products in the same grocery aisle you're in ("*I saw this sauce in an online recipe. Have you tried cooking with it?*"). At the checkout counter, smile and greet the cashier ("*How's your shift going so far?*").

Make it a goal to initiate and create a 10-second interaction with a stranger every day. This will warm you up for interactions, build in you the habit of being interested in people, and boost your social confidence.

As you get into the habit of engaging in short interactions with people, you begin to really see them as individuals—human beings leading their own colorful lives instead of merely instruments or bland life-forms we have no choice but to put up with. You will become more social, ready to strike up conversations not because you're expected to by mere convention, but because it's how you ultimately create more meaning in your life.

<u>Warming Up Physically</u>

Warming yourself up psychologically and getting into the general mood on a daily basis are important aspects of pre-conversation, but just as important is the way you prepare your body. Think of it this way: conversation is a race, and you have to warm up and prepare yourself accordingly.

When we want our best race, whether athletic or academic, we always engage in some type of warm-up. It's almost common sense at this point that you need to prime your body and mind to the kind of performance that you want. Runners stretch, singers sing scales. What about people engaging in conversation? Well, you might be surprised by how much your speaking muscles need help and how much getting them in shape can make you instantly more charismatic. Recall back in grade school when you weren't paying attention, the teacher called on you, and you had to spend five seconds clearing your throat while still sounding meek and awkward because you weren't prepared. That's what we are seeking to eliminate, as well as imbue you with a sense of confidence.

To warm up your conversation skills, you just need to do something we've done almost every day in our lives: **read out loud**.

It sounds simple, but reading out loud this time will be different from any other time you've previously done it because you will have a purpose. I've provided an excerpt from the *Wizard of Oz*, which is in the public domain—for those copyright police out there. If this doesn't pique your interest, you can feel free to find your own excerpt. Just try to make sure there is a multitude of emotions included, preferably with dialogue from different characters. Here it is:

After climbing down from the china wall the travelers found themselves in a disagreeable country, full of bogs and marshes and covered with tall, rank grass. It was difficult to walk without falling into muddy holes, for the grass was so thick that it hid them from sight.

However, by carefully picking their way, they got safely along until they reached solid ground. But here the country seemed wilder than ever, and after a long and tiresome walk through the underbrush they entered another forest, where the trees were bigger and older than any they had ever seen.

"This forest is perfectly delightful," declared the Lion, looking around him with joy. "Never have I seen a more beautiful place."

"It seems gloomy," said the Scarecrow.

"Not a bit of it," answered the Lion. "I should like to live here all my life. See how soft the dried leaves are under your feet and how rich and green the moss is that clings to these old trees. Surely no wild beast could wish a pleasanter home."

"Perhaps there are wild beasts in the forest now," said Dorothy.

"I suppose there are," returned the Lion, "but I do not see any of them about."

They walked through the forest until it became too dark to go any farther. Dorothy and Toto and the Lion lay down to sleep, while the Woodman and the Scarecrow kept watch over them as usual.

Seems like an easy task, right? Go ahead and try to read the above excerpt out loud to yourself. Don't be shy. If you actually did it, you'll notice that you do literally feel warmed up and readier to keep speaking and conversing after just using your vocal cords for a bit. But that's just the beginning. Now comes the instruction.

Pretend like you are reading the excerpt out loud to a class of second graders. Read the excerpt like you're giving a performance in a contest, and the winner is judged on how emotional and ridiculous they can be! Pretend you're a voice actor for a movie trailer and you have only your voice to get a wide range of emotion across. Go over the top as much as possible—which, granted, won't be much at first.

Exaggerate every emotion you can find to the tenth degree. Scream parts of it loudly while whispering softly in other parts. Use different and zany voices for different characters. Make any laughter maniacal, make any rage boiling, make any happiness manic—you get the idea. For that matter, what emotions are you picking up in the text? Even in such a short excerpt, there are emotional high and low points. Create them, and make them sound like climaxes to stretch your range of emotion.

Pay attention to your voice tonality. Are you accustomed to using a monotone? Would someone be able to tell what the character or narrator is thinking or trying to convey by listening to you? Use the excerpt to practice your range of vocal expressiveness—try to embody the term *emotional diversity*. Go ahead and try it for the second time with all this newfound instruction.

Did you hear a difference? Here is some additional instruction: pay attention to your diction and how you enunciate. In a sense, you are literally warming your tongue up so you don't stutter or stumble on your words when you talk to others. This is another reason to have an excerpt with dialogue – the more diversity of the text you are reading, the better warmed up you will be. If you have the habit of muttering like a curmudgeon, put a stop to it and make sure you are speaking clear as a bell.

Pay attention to your breathing. Do you feel like you're running out of breath? It's because your diaphragm is weak and not used to projecting or sounding confident. That's the reason singers put their hands on their stomachs – it's to check that their diaphragms are engaged. Try it and make sure that your stomach is taut and tight.

The point here is to literally breathe life into the words that you are speaking. Those who speak without their diaphragm inevitably come off as quiet, meek, and mouse-like. The better you can project your voice, the wider the emotional range you can create.

Another key element of how you say something is, of course, your pacing—the speed at which you talk. Your speaking speed can either be your friend or undermine what you're trying to say. Rate of speech can imply an emotion all by itself—for instance, when making a big point, you should slow down your pace to allow the impact to be felt. If you use the wrong speed or your pacing is off, a lot of what you have to say can easily be lost or confused and misinterpreted. Pauses additionally can say just as much as an expression through words.

Ready to read through the excerpt one more time? Make sure you're utilizing everything you just read. Now compare your third version to the first version you did without any instruction. That's the difference between warming yourself up and not, and most likely, the first version is how you're coming across the vast majority of the time. Hopefully that's illustrative enough evidence for warming up.

The added bonus is that while you are feeling silly and over the top, you are actually stretching your limits in terms of emotional and vocal expressiveness. The simple act of getting out of your comfort zone, even in private, will stretch your boundaries and make you more expressive and confident-sounding in general. All this from reading out loud? Yes, if done with purpose and deliberation!

The Conversation Résumé

Previous points in this chapter about pre-conversation have centered around your psychology and your physiology. In other words, to hit the ground running and have great conversations, you've got to find ways to put yourself in the mood for them. However, we haven't covered what to actually say yet, have we? This is when we rectify that.

As mentioned before, conversation isn't always about thinking quickly on your feet in the heat of the moment. That's an entirely different skill that can be trained, but what's more easy and useful on a daily basis is to create for yourself a *conversation résumé,* which you can draw from in nearly every conversation.

What the heck does this mean? It means that when you're in the heat of a conversation, and an awkward silence is looming, sometimes we stress and our minds blank completely. We try to think on our feet, but our feet are frozen to the floor. A conversation résumé comes to the rescue because it is an annotated overview of who you are. It's a brief list of your best and funniest stories, your notable accomplishments, your unique experiences, and viewpoints on salient and topical issues. It allows you to keep your best bits ready for usage.

It's no different from a résumé you would use for a job interview—but with a very different purpose in mind here. Know your personal talking points, rehearse them, and be ready to unleash them whenever necessary. However, just like in a job interview, having this résumé allows you to present the version of yourself that you most want.

It may seem inconsequential to have such thoughts prepared, but imagine how excruciating the silence is in a job interview when you have to scramble, think of an answer on the fly, and say it while knowing it's generic or useless. It's simply the difference between having a good answer or story when someone asks "What did you do last weekend?" versus simply saying "Oh, not too much. Some TV. What about you?" How about how few of us can answer the following without stuttering and stalling: "So what's your story?" The conversation résumé allows you to remind yourself that you're not such a boring person after all and that people should have reason to be interested in you.

Developing and constantly updating your conversation résumé can save you from awkward silences and make it supremely easy to connect with others. It may feel difficult to come up with right now, but imagine how much easier it is without the stress of someone staring at you, waiting for your reply. It's this process of mental agony that will translate to real conversational success. What you come up with on your résumé won't always make it into everyday conversation, but the more you have it on your brain, the more it will, and the more captivating you will appear become.

There are four sections to your conversation résumé, and it's not a bad idea to update them every couple of weeks. Admittedly, you may never have thought to answer any of these questions before, which means they definitely aren't coming through in conversation. Don't sell yourself short!

Daily life:
- What did you do over the weekend? Anything notable?
- How is your week/day going? Anything notable?
- How is your family/significant other? Anything notable?
- How is work going? Anything notable?

Personal:
- What are your hobbies? Anything notable?
- What's your biggest passion or interest outside of work? Anything notable?
- Where are you from? Anything notable?
- How long have you lived at your current location and worked at your current job? Anything notable?
- Where did you go to school and what were you involved in? Anything notable?
- What do you do for work? Anything notable?

Notable:

- What are your five most unique experiences?
- What are your five most personally significant accomplishments?
- What are 10 strengths—things you are above average at, no matter how big or small.
- Name 10 places you have traveled in the past five years.
- Name the past five times you have gone out to a social event.
- Name 10 things you cannot live without—don't take this question too literally. It is asking about your interests.

Staying Current:
- What are the top five current events of the week *and* month? Learn the basics and develop an opinion and stance on them.
- What are four funny personal situations from the past week? Be able to summarize them as a brief story.
- What are the four most interesting things you've read or heard about in the past week? Be able to summarize them as a brief story.

If you've ever felt like your mind was going blank, this is the cure. There are so many pieces of information that you've just dug out of yourself that it should be nearly impossible to run out of things to say. Remember to review this before you head into socially intense situations, and you will be able to keep up with just about anyone.

You just may realize that while some people appear to be quicker than lightning, they may simply remember more about themselves at that moment.

Fallback Stories

You can come in with a strong conversation résumé, and that will take care of most issues most people have. But even that sometimes leads conversations down a linear road to boredom and generic-isms. At the very least, you'll probably notice the same lines of questioning and statements when you talk about your unique and interest accomplishments and experiences. Others might be engaged, but you probably won't be at some point.

The conversation résumé was aimed at keeping you sounding interesting—but what about when you want novel information and opinions yourself? Fallback stories can reinvigorate a conversation that was slowly or quickly circling the drain.

Fallback stories, as I like to call them, can be used as fallbacks (duh) when you run out of things to say or want to move a conversation in a completely different direction. If you can see the writing on the wall that your current topic is going to get more and more boring, it's time to use a fallback story. They can be prepared before the conversation, so you can carry it around in your back pocket until you need it. They are actually similar to the last parts of the conversation résumé, as you'll see, in that they reference external events.

A fallback story has four distinct components—it sounds like a lot to process during a conversation, but don't worry: they come fairly naturally and organically once you've had a tiny bit of practice with them. Also, rest assured that a fallback story does not focus on the storytelling itself. It is not the important aspect.

The four components to fallback stories:
- the bridging sentence
- the story itself
- your opinion of the story
- asking for people's opinion in different ways

Illustration is always better, so here's an example. Imagine that a conversation is dying down or there is a lull between topics. In either case, you're not sure what to say at the moment.

(1) Bridging sentence: *Hey, you know what I heard recently?*

(2) The story itself: *One of my female friends just proposed to her boyfriend and now they are engaged. Apparently she just didn't want to keep waiting and decided to be progressive and ignore gender roles and take her life into her own hands. She even had a ring and everything.*

(3) Your opinion: *When I first heard about it, I generally thought "Why not? It's 2016!" I know them both and it kind of suits their*

relationship.

(4) Asking for their opinion: *What do you think about that? Would you ever do that? How would you react if your significant other did that with you? Would you do the ring as well?*

At first glance, this seems like a casual attention-grabbing story that will galvanize conversation because of the way it was presented and the questions that were posed at the end to continue discussion. However, each of the separate components plays an important role in making this happen.

The first component is the bridging sentence. It is short, but it provides a short, plausible transition from whatever the previous topic was into your fallback story. You don't need to say much with it; it just provides context for why you are even bringing it up. You just heard about it recently. Don't overthink this part with protests like "How can you dive into that topic from silence or the former topic?" That's what this bridging sentence does in an easy and quick way.

The second component is the actual story itself. Now, notice that it's not long, and the story details don't even really matter that much here. The story just introduces one or two main premises and I don't go into the nitty-gritty detail because that's not what drives a conversation forward.

I introduce the premises, try to focus on the one or two primary emotions that I want to evoke, and move on from there. It's short, and most storytelling books gum it up and make it too convoluted by introducing formulas for telling a simple story. A story by itself is great, but what happens after is the important part.

The third component is the speaker's opinion on the matter. For most of these fallback stories, you want to provide a positive opinion on it; otherwise, people may not feel comfortable opening up and sharing if they happen to disagree with you. In other words, if I said that I thought it was a terrible decision that the female proposed to the male, the other person may not be able to say they thought it was a good idea for fear of irking or contradicting me. Just share how you feel about it and try to place yourself in the context.

This component is key to opening the other person up, because you've shared first and made yourself vulnerable. The other person will feel safer after you've disclosed your position first—that's just a facet of human psychology.

The fourth and final component seems like a series of inane questions, but there is logic to the chaos. When you ask someone to generally comment on a situation, most people have a tough time with it because it is so open-ended and broad. They have an infinite choice of directions to go and they aren't sure the exact question you were asking.

"Would I do that? What do you mean? Propose at all? If I were a woman, or as a man? I don't understand the question you're asking."

Thus, fallback stories are best when concluded with a series of questions. The reason is that the type of answer you are looking for becomes clear when you ask a series of questions, and different questions will resonate with different people. So the person you're speaking to might not really understand or have anything to say about the first three questions but will light up upon hearing the fourth question—even if it is essentially the same question posed in a different way.

The reason I know this approach with a series of questions works is because you can physically see people's faces light up when you ask a question that resonates with them and when they have something to answer with—again, even if it's the same exact question worded differently.

Those are the four components of a good fallback story—and again, the best part about these is you can prepare them beforehand and carry them in your sleeve whenever you feel you need to spice things up conversationally. Conversation has the distinct ability to drain us of our confidence because we never know what twists and turns we'll hit. Mining your life for fallback stories can help create just a bit more predictability and security.

Does the above story seem like a good one? It works because it's an interpersonal situation with universal themes and questions—which means that essentially everyone can have an opinion on it.

When you are thinking of what fallback stories to pack into your sleeve, interpersonal situations tend to work for that reason. Other prompts that make good fallback stories are asking people what they would do in certain hypothetical situations, and asking for opinions on moral dilemmas (as long as they aren't dark and depressing). You're going for universal themes above all else, because that's when you can ensure that people will have something to add to the ensuing discussion; otherwise, it will just turn into you telling a story about an interesting occurrence.

For example:

- My friend spent $300 on a meal, mostly on wine, for no apparent occasion or reason. In what circumstances would you

spend $300 on a meal?
- My friend saw his friend's significant other cheating on his friend. He told his friend. Would you tell?
- Someone took a $40,000 USD pay cut to work at their dream job. Where is the line for you?
- Someone found out they had two weeks to live and went to Antarctica. Does that sound attractive to you, or would you do something completely different?

Just remember to phrase these all into stories that seem to have randomly popped into your head, provide your opinion on it, and ask for their opinion in various ways.

The pre-conversation stage can take many appearances, and there are ways of preparing physically, psychologically, and practically for what's to come.

Takeaways:

- Great conversations start before the actual conversation in the sense that there are many things you should do to prepare yourself to be charming and

witty.
- You can get yourself ready for the interaction by warming up beforehand—psychologically and physically. Psychologically is a matter of getting in the mood to socialize and also becoming used to initiating interaction. This can be done with "10-second relationships," which plunge you into the deep end if only for a moment. Physically, you should seek to warm up by reading out loud before socializing and making sure you exaggerate emotional expressiveness and variation. Read out loud three times and notice the difference in engagement, and you can instantly see the contrast of how you might come off.
- An additional way of preparing before conversations is to get your own information and life in order, and this can be done by following a conversation résumé. The purpose is to draw into your past and find what makes you an interesting person and make sure that is all at the tip of your tongue for easy usage.
- Fallback stories also have the same purpose. If you can create a fallback story, which has four simple components

(bridge, story, your opinion, their opinion), you can walk into a conversation knowing that you can handle any awkward silence or topic change.

Chapter 2. Setting the Tone

Most people don't barrel into conversation head-first. Rather, they gently dip a toe in and test the waters. If you've never met someone before, you naturally feel like you need to feel them out and understand how they interact with people and generally how loose and appropriate you can be.

For instance, remember when you were in elementary school and you found out you would have a substitute teacher the next day? It was a scary moment for most, unless you hated your normal teacher. It was scary because you never knew how strict or vicious the substitute would be, and you would have to be on your best behavior for a few days until you figured them out.

The next morning, suppose the substitute teacher walks in with impeccable posture and addresses everyone as "mister" and "miss" even though you are eight years old. That's the tone they chose to set, which is obviously not ideal for you. But what if the substitute teacher were to walk in with an untucked shirt and sandals and immediately address the class as "buddies" and "dudes"? I'm not saying one is superior to the other, but a tone is clearly being set by each of these teachers.

In conversations, people size you up in the same way. They look at how you carry yourself, and they are waiting for a sign that it's okay for them to be more relaxed and personable around you. More specifically, they want signs they can relax and let their hair down, so to speak. Knowing this, you should be cognizant of setting the tone with others. You may want to wait for a sign from them, but it's this too often causes a game of chicken where no one wants to make the first move.

Simply, we are keeping ourselves from conversational success by talking like strangers and acting as if you aren't yet friends. Setting the tone means making the mental leap to "we're friends now" and treating them as such.

<u>Speak Like Friends</u>

At the most basic level, this means to speak like friends and stop speaking to everyone like you've just met them at a professional networking event. How do friends speak, exactly? It might feel like we've overanalyzed things to the point that you've forgotten the difference.

I had one of the most interesting conversations of the year a couple months ago, and you'll never guess who the other party was. Let me first tell you why exactly the conversation was so good. I did most of the talking, and filling the air with your own voice is pretty gratifying.

This means that it wasn't particularly what my conversation partner said to me; it was the approach she had. My conversation partner essentially had no filter. This was refreshing, as most day-to-day banter can be uniform and vanilla. The lack of a filter means it will go places that are interesting, emotion-driven, and somewhat inappropriate.

Of course, the best topics are always inappropriate. Very few topics are truly inappropriate—you just have to speak about those topics in an appropriate manner.

My conversation partner was also very direct and lacked any pretense or tact. She got straight to the point and any excuses or justifications I provided for my reasoning were shot down—some deservedly so. I could rationalize them to myself, but they didn't make sense to her, and she said it. Two plus two only equaled four, and nothing else could impact it. Speaking to someone who wasn't afraid of beating around the bush for the sake of social norms was refreshing. They weren't afraid of asking the deep and tough questions, no matter how often she had to ask "but why?" to understand something. Often, it went down a hole that others would have avoided. She had to ask a few times before I readily admitted and opened up.

Finally, along with that lack of pretense for me was a lack of pretense for her. There was no judgment, and it was apparent that everything was motivated by sheer, genuine curiosity. It made me feel acceptable being vulnerable and sharing my more private thoughts.

You got me—the conversation partner was an eight-year-old I met at an acquaintance's barbecue. For most of us, we have trouble with conversation when we think about it too much. We analyze in our head, attempt to plan, and unnecessarily filter what we have to say. No matter how exciting or emotionally engaging the thoughts swimming around our noodle may be, what makes it out of our mouths can be downright dull. We stick to the tried and proven safe topics. We filter out the excitement and intrigue because we don't want to rile any feathers or because we are self-conscious ourselves.

Children do not have this problem, and that's the tone they set. This is always the choice you have as well.

They speak completely without filters and a lack of knowledge about what is socially acceptable and what is not. They spontaneously blurt out the first thing that comes to mind. That's how friends speak.

Take a second and try to access your memory banks as to how you would have approached conversations as a child. You didn't have a filter, you showed emotions, and you said what was on your mind. Similarly, you would have had no problem "going there."

Children haven't quite developed the self-awareness to know when they are offending people. Have you ever been around a child when someone with a birth defect walks by? The child will usually be mystified and fascinated, staring with impunity.

They are not shy and aren't afraid to keep asking questions, despite the rabbit hole they might slither down. They just don't know better and want a satisfactory answer to their questions and curiosity. They don't care about the "appropriateness" adults get hung up on.

The reason most adults pull back is because we feel embarrassed or we're afraid of making the other person feel embarrassed. The vast majority of the time, our fears are highly unjustified. Again, is this the way you'd speak to a stranger or to a good friend? Which is better for our purposes of making friends?

Find Similarity

Think back to the last time you met someone new at a networking event or party. What was the first topic out of your mouth? It was probably one of the following:

- Where are you from?
- Who do you know here?
- How was your weekend?
- Where did you go to school?
- What do you do?

While these are normal small talk questions, we ask them instinctively not because they are great at breaking the ice. In fact, as you well know, they are usually terrible for breaking the ice and can make people feel immediately bored.

We actually ask them instinctively because we are searching for commonalities. We are searching for the "me too!" moment that can spark a deeper discussion. For instance, if we ask the question "Where did you go to school?" we are hoping they attended the same university as us or a university where we have mutual friends. The next natural question we always ask is a variation of "Oh wow! What a small world. Do you know James Taylor? He also went there around your time."

While you may not realize that, you are always hunting for similarities, and similarities are another way of setting a tone of friendship, familiarity, comfort, and openness. It's the type of feeling you share with your friends, and the same feeling that can instantly skyrocket your rapport.

As much as we would like to think that we are open-minded and can get along with people from every background and origin, the reality is that we usually get along best with people who we think are like us. In fact, we seek them out.

It's why places like Little Italy, Chinatown, and Koreatown exist.

But I'm not just talking about race, skin color, religion, or sexual orientation. I'm talking about people who share our values, look at the world the same way we do, and have the same take on things as we do. As the saying goes, birds of a feather flock together. This is a very common human tendency that is rooted in how our species developed. Walking out on the tundra or in a forest, you would be conditioned to avoid that which is unfamiliar or foreign because there is a high likelihood it would be interested in killing you.

Similarities make us relate better to other people because we think they'll understand us on a deeper level than other people. If we share at least one significant similarity, then all sorts of positive traits follow, because we see them as our contemporary, essentially an extension of ourselves. When you think someone is on your level, you want to connect with them because they will probably understand you better than most.

Suppose you were born in a small village in South Africa. The population of the village ranges from 900 to 1000 people. You now live in London and you are attending a party at a friend's home. You meet someone that also happens to be from that small village in South Africa, just eight years older so you never encountered each other.

What warm feelings will you immediately have toward this other person, and what assumptions will you make about them? How interested will you be in connecting with them and spending more time together in the future? What inside jokes or specialized points of reference can you discuss that you haven't been able to with anyone else, ever?

Hopefully that illustration drives home the value of similarity and how it drives conversational connection.

We typically use the small talk questions I mentioned at the top of this chapter to find similarity, but there are better, more effective ways to find similarities with people. For instance, we should always be *searching* for similarities or *creating* them. They both take effort and initiative.

We can *search* for similarities by asking probing questions of people and using their answers as the basis to show similarity, no matter how small. Ask questions to figure out what people are about, what they like, and how they think. Then dig deep into yourself to find small commonalities at first, such as favorite baseball teams or alcoholic drinks. Through those smaller commonalities, you'll be able to figure out what makes them tick and find deeper commonalities to instantly bond over. Just as you'd be thrilled to meet someone from that small South African town, you'd be thrilled to meet someone who shared a love of the same obscure hobby as you.

It doesn't take months or years, and it doesn't take a special circumstance like going through boot camp together. It just requires you to look outside of yourself and realize that people share common attitudes, experiences, and emotions—you just have to find them. Get comfortable asking questions and digging deeper than you naturally would. (Is it odd for you to ask five questions in a row? It shouldn't be.) It might even feel a little invasive at first. Find them and use them!

We can *create* similarities by mimicking people's body language, voice tonality, rate of speech, and overall manner of appearance. This is known as *mirroring*, and it has also been shown to produce feelings of positivity when tested (Anderson, 1998). All you have to do is arrange yourself to resemble others in order to benefit from feelings of similarity, from how they are posed to how they gesture.

You can mirror their words, their tone of voice, and their mannerisms. Keep in mind that mirroring is not just about reflecting them on a wholesale basis. Instead, it is all about communicating to them that you share similar values and have the potential to connect intimately.

You can mirror physical signals, gestures,

tics, and mannerisms. For example, if you notice that someone uses a lot of gestures when talking, you should do the same. Similarly, if you notice that someone's body language involves a lot of leaning and crossing of arms, you should do the same.

You can mirror their verbal expressions and expressiveness—tone of voice, inflection, word choice, slang and vocabulary, emotional intonation, and excitement and energy.

Similarities are easier to find when you share personal information and divulge details.

Statement one: You went skiing last month. Statement two: You went skiing last month with your two brothers and you almost broke your foot.

Which of those stories is easier to relate to and find a similarity with? Obviously, the second version since there is literally three times as much information. If you are having trouble connecting with others, it's likely you are expecting to find a similarity without sharing anything yourself.

If sharing even this amount of detail feels uncomfortable and unnatural for you, it's a sign you probably don't give your conversation partners much to work with and you are essentially dropping the conversational ball when it is hit back to you. You may be the cause of awkward silence more often than not, because others will expect a back and forth flow, but they end up doing all the work while you wonder what's wrong.

In other words, get used to this feeling of discomfort because it's something you need to improve upon.

Mutual dislike is just as good as a similarity and might even be more fun. Have you noticed that it is sometimes inevitable for the conversation to remain positive, and the conversation will veer into a set of complaints about something you both dislike?

It's easy to discount these discussions because people think talking about negativity is a negative thing. However, it's absolutely valuable in your quest for connection because negativity and hate is a strong, powerful emotion.

When you check out a new restaurant, think about the reviews you'll read about it. You'll either read highly positive, gushing reviews or, more likely, the negative reviews filled with hate and spite. Hatred moves us into action like nothing else.

Some relationship counselors have even gone so far as to quip that a sign of highly successful relationships is the ability to hate the same things and people.

It's not negative to talk about negativity because it's an emotion like any other, and the more emotion you can generate in your interaction, the greater an impression you will make.

What's ultimately important is seeing eye to eye once again. How many friendships have been built in army boot camps, where the singular common bond was a hatred for the suffering they went through? How many friendships have been built on the back of hating the same teacher or morning schedule? You've bonded over common dislike far more often than you realize, so you shouldn't stray away from it.

<u>Strategically Swear</u>

"Your record collection is so fucking cool!" you blurt out to a colleague whose house party you're attending. For a split-second, there's only silence between the two of you. You hesitate and think to yourself, *"Did I offend him by the language I used?"* He stares at you. You stare at him. You feel a little quickening of your heartbeat, your breath catching.

Then his face breaks into a smile and he responds in kind with a profanity-laced spike of excitement.

How do you think you'd feel after that exchange? Chances are, you'll have felt closer or at least more comfortable relating to your colleague more openly. Why is this so? Isn't swearing, being a taboo act, something that generally makes people uncomfortable and is maybe even alienating to some?

Maybe in some instances it is. But as you've seen in the above scenario (or may have experienced yourself), there are occasions when swearing could actually bring two people closer with one another. Our understanding of the role of swearing in human interaction is thus now beginning to shift, from being strictly a no-no act in civilized interactions to now being an endorsed approach for deepening a bond with someone. How is it possible that something considered taboo is the same thing that'll help us build better relationships with the people around us?

As discussed by Michael Adams in his book *In Praise of Profanity*, the psychology behind the phenomenon of swearing as a relational catalyst is this: it's precisely the taboo nature of swearing that gives it the power to build intimacy between people. Because we're well aware of the fact that we're not supposed to do it, we also understand the risk involved in doing it in front of someone, especially someone we know so little about. We never know how they're going to react—are they going to accept it, tolerate it, avoid it, or despise it?

Putting ourselves in this position where we're just as likely to be rejected as accepted is an act of letting our guard down. This, in turn, lets the other person know it's okay to let their guard down with us as well. When we swear, we show them we're comfortable enough to release our raw, in-the-moment emotions in front of them, so they're likely to ease up on their own defenses and relate to us in like manner.

Say you're holding an orientation with the company's new hires. You sense tension in the room. They're all looking at you with an air of cautious detachment, as if trying to sense whether you bite or punish people for smiling and chatting willy-nilly. Instead of letting the room simmer in unease as you deliver the orientation in a deadpan manner, how about breaking the ice by throwing a couple of swearwords in there at apt moments?

While explaining the dress code, instead of the just delivering the stern "*The company does not allow the wearing of clothes that are too revealing,*" you might add, "*Who the fuck goes to work in see-through blouses and spandex tights?"* You'll get chuckles and maybe even a few witty comebacks from around the room, breaking the tension and allowing people to relax and show their personalities a bit more. By swearing, you'll avoid coming across as an uptight superior and instead be seen as an easygoing, relatable mate. People will relax around you, and that's the first step to building a relationship.

By showing unfiltered emotion and vulnerability, swearing breaks the ice, instantly builds rapport, and starts you off to a more intimate connection with others. It shows genuineness, honesty, transparency, and vulnerability. So the next time you're with an acquaintance you want to get closer with, test the waters by letting slip a couple of profanities. To express a spirited agreement, say "*Fuck yeah*" instead of the formal "*I agree.*" To express disagreement, try inserting "*Bitch, please*" in there somewhere. Once you start using curse words in front of each other without having to worry that you'll be rejected for it, it's when shit gets real between the two of you.

Talking

One last tip for this chapter on setting a tone of openness and friendliness. Some people just aren't very forthcoming. It can be annoying. They can be like talking to walls for no apparent reason. You can ask them something seemingly innocent, and they just dodge, demur, or give you a one-word answer. Or you ask something juicy, and they try to keep changing the subjects. You might have violated their privacy, or they might just be too protective. Whatever the case, conversation has now come to a full stop.

Unfortunately, they have set the tone to treat you as a stranger and hold you at arm's length, which is something we are making sure we don't do ourselves. But that's okay, this is something you can sneakily move past to crack people open. How?

When you ask a question you think may not be answered, act as if they answered it and react to that hypothetical answer.

You: So I hear that project didn't go so well at work?
Bob: Yeah. Not great.
You: Yeah, I heard things were going excellent minus that little snafu at the end of the quarter. But that's no one's fault. That part of the project is super complex. It's crazy. I can't believe it even got the green light.

When you put all of this on the table, it's going to be nearly irresistible for them to step in and answer, reply, correct, confirm, or deny. That's the important part—you are (1) asking a question, (2) acting as if *they* answered the question, and (3) then seeing how they react to your assumption of their answer. Don't wait for them to react to your question; just wait for them to react to your subsequent answer. The premise here is that even if they don't want to talk to you, they'll be forced to engage and step in to intervene in some way. You may not get the merriest of answers, but the important part is that you've gotten them to open their traps in the first place, and that can be the hardest part of all.

There's another variation on this way of getting people to engage or otherwise speak up. *When you ask someone a question, assume they are going to answer a certain way and keep elaborating on that sentiment.* Again, if you're lucky, people will feel compelled to correct you and clarify what their actual answer to the question is.

You: So how was the vacation? I bet it was terrible with all of those worms and alligators. I hate the water and humidity so much.
Bobby: Well, actually…

Gotcha! In the same vein, you can elicit people to speak and open up more by talking about something you know is obviously wrong and waiting for them to jump in.

You: That relationship seemed so good because he has a nice car right? That's all you need. I guess when it's a Corvette it's enough. Money is life.
Bobbi: Well, actually…

These methods capitalize on people's instinct to set the record straight. Even if they don't want to talk about something, they don't want the incorrect or negative perception floating around about them. If you were only getting one word out of them, and you are able to get two sentences out of them by using this tactic, consider it a win to keep building on.

Remember that the tone is something you have 100% ability to set. Many of us feel that conversations are a matter of luck—you strike it lucky by finding a mutual topic of interest or similarity, and those instances are necessary to create rapport. Of course, if you believe this to be the case, it *will* be the case for you.

Takeaways:

- What determines whether you hit it off with someone? It's not circumstantial; rather, it's a matter of you taking charge and setting the tone to be friendly and open. Most people treat others like strangers and thus won't become friends.
- The first way to set the tone then is to

speak like friends: topic-wise, tone-wise, and even privacy-wise. People will go along with the tone you set as long as you aren't outright offensive. A powerful aspect of this is showing unfiltered emotion with people as friends do instead of filtering yourself and putting up a wall for the literal purpose of keeping people at a distance. Yes, this includes swearing and getting people to let their guards down.

- Another aspect of setting the right tone is to find and focus on similarities. When people observe similarity, they instantly open up and embrace it because it is a reflection of themselves. You can do this by creating similarities or digging for similarities.
- Finally, you can set the tone by getting people to talk even when they are closed off or seem intent on keeping you at an arm's length. You can do this by asking specific questions that are irresistible for them to either comment on, explain, or defend—the questions aren't necessarily for them to actually answer.

Chapter 3. How to Be Captivating

What comes to mind when you think of a captivating conversationalist? More often than not, I would bet that you would think of someone who is great at storytelling. It seems that only with storytelling can we mesmerize and charm others into hanging onto our every word.

Whether or not that is true is not the aim of this chapter. No one can deny that storytelling is an important element of memorable conversations and conversations that you want to have. The question is always how to capture this elusive skill and make it your own. Therefore, in this chapter, I want to present a few perspectives on how you can use storytelling in your everyday conversations.

It's productive to first take the mystique away from the whole concept of storytelling. What is storytelling? It's just relating something that happened in a way that isn't boring and that makes you the center of attention for a bit. That's all. With that in mind, let's see how we can get better at storytelling.

Life Is a Series of Stories

No, seriously. We don't think of our lives as being very interesting on a day to day basis, but we do quite a bit more than we realize.

This proposition, combined with the fact that nothing stops a conversation cold quite like a one-word answer, means that you should strive to make your life a series of mini stories. Keep in mind that we're taking the mystique out of stories, and you'll find that it's easy to create mini stories about every day of your life.

What is the definition of a mini story in this

context?

"So what do you do?"
"I'm a marketing executive."
"Oh, cool. Well, I'm going to find the bathroom now."

Let's try again.

"So what do you do?"
"I'm a marketing executive. I deal mostly with clients. Just last week we had a crazy client that threatened to send his bodyguards to our office! I definitely wish I dealt more with the creative side."
"Oh my God! Did he actually send them?"

That's a mini story. It's answering questions briefly using the elements of a story—an action that occurs to a subject with some sort of conclusion. As you can see above, a brief mini story will create exponentially more conversation and interest than any answer to the question "What do you do?" All you needed was three sentences. And this is all you need to make yourself an exponentially more captivating conversationalist. When people make small talk with you and ask your small talk questions, they probably aren't interested in your one-word answers or boring recaps of boring weekends. They want to hear something interesting, so give it to them.

Not only that, stories are an inside view to the way you think and feel. Learning those about you is the first step in allowing anyone to relate and feel connected to you, so it's imperative that you learn how to take a closed-ended question and expand it to your advantage. It will also encourage them to reciprocate, and suddenly trading war stories from college parties is on the table. When you break down what a mini story actually needs, they become much simpler.

What's great about mini stories is you can also create these before a conversation so you can have compelling anecdotes at hand in response to very common and widespread questions. The main benefit to creating mini stories ahead of time is to be able to avoid one-word answers that you may be accustomed to using.

I would implore you to cue up similar mini

stories of roughly three sentences in length for some of the most common conversation topics that will arise, such as:

1. Your occupation (if you have a job that is unusual or nebulous, make sure that you have a layman's description of your job that people can relate to)
2. Your week
3. Your upcoming weekend
4. Your hometown
5. Your hobbies and so on.

When you are using a mini story to answer a question, make sure to first acknowledge the question that was asked. But then, realizing that you have something far more interesting to say, you can jump into the mini story, which should be able to stand by itself.

"How was your weekend?"
"It was fine. I watched four Star Wars movies."
"Okay, I'm going to go talk to someone else now."

Let's try again.

"How was your weekend?"
"It was fine, but did I tell you about what happened last weekend? A dog wearing a tuxedo walked into my office."
"Wait. Tell me more."

Using mini stories allows you to avoid the tired back of forth of "Good, how about you" you'll find in everyday small talk. That's the first step to being captivating.

Mini stories also underscore the importance of providing more details, as mentioned in an earlier chapter, and avoiding one-word answers.

Details provide a three-dimensional description of you and your life. That automatically makes people more interested and invested because they are already painting a mental picture in their minds and visualizing everything.

Details also give people more to connect to, think about, and attach themselves to. With more details, there is a substantially higher likelihood that people will find something funny, interesting, in common, poignant, curious, and worthy of comment.

Detail and specificity put people into a specific place and time. It allows them to imagine exactly what's happening and start caring about it. Think about why it's so easy to get sucked into a movie. We experience enormous sensory stimulation and almost can't escape all of the visual and auditory detail, which is designed to make us invested. Detailed stories and conversations are inviting others to share a mental movie with you.

Beyond giving flavor to your conversation and storytelling, and giving the other person something to ask about, details are important because they are what make people emotionally engaged. Details remind people of their own lives and memories and make them feel more drawn to whatever is presenting them. Details can compel others to laugh, feel mad, feel sad, or feel surprise. They can control moods and emotions.

If you include details about specific songs that played during your high school dances, it's likely that someone will have memories attached to those songs and become more emotionally interested in your story. There is no such thing as TMI—too much information. Share details about all the figurative nooks and crannies, because that's what makes you interesting on an emotional level.

The 1:1:1 Method

On the theme of simplifying storytelling, we've been talking about how we can use a mini story in many ways. You may be wondering what the difference is between a *mini* story and a *full-fledged* story.

To me, not much. As I mentioned, many people like to complicate storytelling as if they were composing an impromptu Greek tragedy. Does there have to be an introduction, middle, struggle, then resolution? You may have read that great stories are about X, Y, and Z; that you need a beginning, middle, and ending; that you should use as much descriptive detail as possible; or how important pauses are. That's one way of doing it, but certainly not the easiest or most practical.

My method of storytelling in conversation is

to prioritize the discussion afterward—similar to what you saw with the fallback stories in an earlier chapter. This means that the story itself doesn't need to be that in-depth or long. It can and should contain specific details that people can relate to and latch onto, but it doesn't need to have parts or stages. It can be *mini* by nature. That's why it's called the *1:1:1 method*.

It stands for a story that (1) has one action, (2) can be summed up in one sentence, and (3) evokes one primary emotion in the listener. You can see why they're short and snappy. They also tend to make sure that you know your point before starting and have a very low chance of verbally wandering for minutes and alienating your listeners.

For a story to consist of *one action* means only one thing is happening. The story is about one occurrence. It should be direct and straightforward. Anything else just confuses the point and makes you liable to ramble.

A story should be able to be *summed up* in one sentence because, otherwise, you are trying to convey too much. This step actually takes practice, because you are forced to think about which aspects matter and which don't add anything to your action. It's a skill to be able to distill your thoughts into one sentence and still be thorough—often, you won't realize what you want to say unless you can do this.

Finally, a story should focus on one primary emotion to be evoked in the listener. And you should be able to name it! Keep in mind that evoking an emotion ensures that your story actually has a point, and it will color what details you carefully choose to emphasize that emotion. For our purposes here, there really aren't that many emotions you might want to evoke in others from a story. You might have humor, shock, awe, envy, happiness, anger, or annoyance. Those are the majority of reasons we relate our experiences to others.

Keep in mind that it's just my method for conveying my experiences to others. Whether people hear two sentences about a dog attack or they hear 10 sentences doesn't change the impact of the story. The reason I abbreviate stories is so the conversation can move forward and we can then focus on the listener's impact and reaction. So what does this so-called story sound like?

"I was attacked by a dog and I was so frightened I nearly wet my pants." It's one sentence, there is one action, and the bit about wetting the pants is to emphasize the fact that the emotion you want to convey is fear and shock.

You could include more detail about the dog and the circumstances, but chances are people are going to ask about that immediately, so let them guide what they want to hear about your story. Invite them to participate! Very few people want to sit and listen to a monologue, most of which is told poorly and in a scattered manner. Therefore, keep the essentials but cut your story short, and let the conversation continue as a shared experience rather than you monopolizing the airspace. Make it a shared experience rather than all about you.

The 1:1:1 method can be summed up as starting a story as close to the end as possible. Most stories end before they get to the end, in terms of impact on the listener, their attention span, and the energy that you have to tell it. In other words, many stories tend to drone on because people try to adhere to these rules or because they simply lose the plot and are trying to find it again through talking. Above all else, a long preamble is not necessary. What's important is that people pay attention, care, and will react in some (preferably) emotional manner.

Ask for Stories

Most of the focus with stories is usually on telling them—but what about soliciting them from others and allowing them to feel as good as you do when a story lands well? What about stepping aside and giving other people the spotlight? Well, it's just a matter of how you ask for them.

When you watch sports, one of the most illogical parts is the post-game or post-match interview. These athletes are still caught in the throes of adrenaline, out of breath, and occasionally drip sweat onto the reporters.

Yet when you are watching a broadcaster interview an athlete, does anything odd strike you about the questions they ask? The interviewers are put into an impossible situation and usually walk away with decent soundbites—at the very least, not audio disasters. Their duty is to elicit a coherent answer from someone who is mentally incoherent at the moment. How do they do that?

They'll ask questions like "So tell me about that moment in the second quarter. What did you feel about it and how did the coach turn it around then?" as opposed to "How'd you guys win?" or "How did you turn this match around, come back, and pull out all the stops to grab the victory at the very end?" as opposed to "How was the comeback?"

The key? They ask for a story rather than an answer. They phrase their inquiry in a way that can only be answered with a story, in fact.

Detail, context, and boundaries are given for the athletes to set them up to talk as much as possible instead of providing a breathless one-word answer. It's almost as if they provide the athletes with an outline of what they want to hear and how they can proceed. They make it easy for them to tell a story and simply engage. It's like if someone asks you a question but, in the question, tells you exactly what they want to hear as hints.

Sometimes we think we are doing the heavy lifting in a conversation and the other party isn't giving us much to work with. But that's a massive cop-out. They might not be giving you much, but you also might be asking them the wrong questions, which is making them give you terrible responses. In fact, if you think you are shouldering the burden, you are definitely asking the wrong questions.

Conversation can be much more pleasant for everyone involved if you provide fertile ground for people to work in. Don't set the other person up to fail and be a poor conversationalist; that will only make you invest and care less and cause the conversation to die out.

When people ask me low-effort, vague questions, I know they probably aren't interested in the answer. They're just filling the time and silence. To create win-win conversations and better circumstances for all, ask for stories the way the sports broadcasters do. Ask questions in a way that makes people want to share.

Stories are personal, emotional, and compelling. There is a thought process and narrative that necessarily exists. They are what show your personality and are how you can learn about someone. They show people's emotions and how they think. Last but not least, they show what you care about.

Compare this with simply asking for closed-ended answers. Answers are often too boring and routine for people to care. They will still answer your questions but in a very literal way, and the level of engagement won't be there. Peppering people with shallow questions puts people in a position to fail conversationally.

It's the difference between asking "What was the best part of your day so far? Tell me how you got that parking space so close!" instead of just "How are you?"

When you ask somebody the second question, you're asking for a quick, uninvolved answer. You're being lazy and either don't care about their answer or want them to carry the conversational burden. When you ask somebody one of the first two questions, you're inviting them to tell a specific story about their day. You are inviting them to narrate the series of events that made their day great or not. And it can't really be answered with a one-word answer.

Another example is "What is the most exciting part of your job? How does it feel to make a difference like that?" instead of simply asking them the generic "What do you do?" When you only ask somebody what they do for a living, you know exactly how the rest of the conversation will go: "Oh, I do X. What about you?"

A final example is "How did you feel about your weekend? What was the best part? It was so nice outside" instead of just "How was your weekend?"

Prompting others for stories instead of

simple answers gives them a chance to speak in such a way that they feel emotionally invested. This increases the sense of meaning they get from the conversation you're having with them. It also makes them feel you are genuinely interested in hearing their answer because your question doesn't sound generic.

Consider the following guidelines when asking a question:

1. Ask for a story
2. Be broad but with specific directions or prompts
3. Ask about feelings and emotions
4. Give the other person a direction to expand their answer into, and give them multiple prompts, hints, and possibilities
5. If all else fails, directly ask "Tell me the story about…"

Imagine that you want the other person to inform your curiosity. Other examples include the following:

1. "Tell me about the time you…" versus "How was that?"
2. "Did you like that…" versus "How was it?"

3. "You look focused. What happened in your morning..." versus "How are you?"

Let's think about what happens when you elicit (and provide) personal stories instead of the old, tired automatic replies.

You say hello to your coworker on Monday morning and you ask how his weekend was. At this point, you have cataloged what you will say in case he asks you the same. Remember, they probably don't care about the actual answer ("good" or "okay"), but they *would* like to hear something interesting. But you never get the chance, because you ask him "How was your weekend? Tell me about the most interesting part—I know you didn't just watch a movie at home!"

He opens up and begins to tell you about his Saturday night when he separately and involuntarily visited a strip joint, a funeral, and a child's birthday party. That's a conversation that can take off and get interesting, and you've successfully bypassed the unnecessary and boring small talk that plagues so many of us.

Most people love talking about themselves. Use this fact to your advantage. Once someone takes your cue and starts sharing a story, make sure you are aware of how you're responding to that person through your facial expressions, gestures, body language, and other nonverbal signals. Since there is always at least one exciting thing in any story, focus on that exciting point and don't be afraid to show that you're engaged.

One quick tip to show that you're engaged and even willing to add is something I call *pinning the tail on the donkey*. There is probably a better name for it, but my vocabulary was severely lacking at the time. The donkey is the story from someone else, while the tail is your addition to it. It allows you to feel like you're contributing, it makes other people know you're listening, and it turns into something you've created together.

People will actually love you for it because, when you do this, your mindset becomes focused on assisting people's stories and letting them have the floor.

Bob's story: "I went to the bank and tripped and spilled all my cash, making it rain inadvertently."

Tail: "Did you think you were Scrooge McDuck for a second?"

When you make a tail, try to hone in on the primary emotion the story was conveying, then add a comment that amplifies it. The story was about how Bob felt rich, and Scrooge McDuck is a duck who swims in pools of gold doubloons, so it adds to the story and doesn't steal Bob's thunder. Get into the habit of assisting other people's stories. It's easy, witty, and extremely likable because you are helping them out.

Use Stories to Create Inside Jokes

In any conversation, there is a high point. There might be multiple memorable points, but by default, one part is the best and highest.

This can take many different forms. You can share a big laugh. You can both get emotional and cry. You share a strong perspective on an issue that no one else does. You witness something either horrifying or hilarious together. You both struggle to not laugh when you observe something. You finish each other's sentences. Most of the time, if you do it correctly, your stories become high points because of the emotional impact and pure intrigue you can use them to create. This makes it easy because you are planting the seed for you to harvest later.

Coincidentally, calling back to this high point later is what a deconstructed inside joke looks like. Therefore, to easily create an inside joke, all you have to do is refer to the high point later in the conversation. Take note of it and put it in your pocket for use in the near future. Don't let it go old like month-old milk that you're afraid to throw away because of the smell. Assuming that you told a good story or elicited a good story earlier in the conversation, all you need to do is refer to it in the context of your current topic.

For example, you told a story about your favorite kind of dog earlier in the conversation. There was a high point about comparing yourself to a wiener dog because your shape makes it unavoidable.

Now your current topic of conversation is style and different types of jackets. How do you call back to the wiener dog high point from earlier by referring to it in the context of jackets? *"Yeah, unfortunately, I can't wear that type of jacket because I'm mostly similar to the wiener dog, remember?"*

Bring up the first topic, hopefully the topic of your story, and then use it in the current topic. Here's another example.

Prior high point: a story about hating parking lots.

Current topic of conversation: the weather.

Callback: *Yeah, the rain will definitely be welcome when we can't find parking spots within ten blocks of our apartment.*

In the same way an orchestra conductor can hit the same high musical motif through different arrangements and songs, you can keep referring to this conversation high point. Voila, you've just created an inside joke from thin air.

Takeaways:

- Captivating people usually refers to telling a story that leaves them listening like children. But there are many ways of creating this feeling in small, everyday ways. Storytelling is a big topic that is often made overly complex.
- An easy way to imagine everyday storytelling is that your life is a series of stories. Instead of giving one-word answers, get into the habit of framing your answers as a story with a point. It creates more engagement, lets you show your personality, and creates smoother conversation. The bonus here is that you can prepare these before a conversation.
- The 1:1:1 method of storytelling is to simplify it as much as possible. The impact of a story won't necessarily be stronger if it is 10 sentences versus two sentences. Therefore, the 1:1:1: method focuses on the discussion and reaction that occurs after a story. A story can be composed solely of (1) one action, (2) one

emotion to be evoked, and (3) a one-sentence summary.
- Telling stories is important, but what about eliciting them from others? You can phrase your questions carefully to ask for stories rather than answers from people, which is a simple way make conversation easier and more enjoyable for everyone involved.
- Stories can also be the basis for an inside joke. When you think about it, an inside joke is something that comes up multiple times with the same person and evokes a positive emotion. Thus, you just need to call back to a story through a conversation and there's a good chance it will stick as a "Remember when we talked about..." moment.

Chapter 4. Charm Offensive

Remember when you had to meet your significant other's parents? Then you instantly understand the meaning of this chapter's title. A charm offensive is most typically used in the context of politicians attempting to win over voters or make up for some type of scandal. "Looks like Senator Johnson was caught with a pool boy. He better go on the charm offensive this next month."

They know they are being held to intense scrutiny, so they reply with intense flattery, positivity, and attention. It's like a blitzkrieg of smiles and compliments. Obviously there are other applications of the charm offensive, and for most of us, it merely refers to when we want to make an impression on someone akin to your in-laws or supervisors. It's slightly different than being likable through normal conversation—here, you are using charming flattery to your advantage.

And no, it's not manipulative unless you use it in such a way.

Compliments

One of the easiest ways to mount a charm offensive is of course to compliment quickly and freely. This is ground zero for flattery and making people light up with a smile about themselves. If you think about it, you probably have positive thoughts about people running through your head all day, so there's no reason to simply give voice to them. We just tend to fixate on sneer-worthy aspects more than we like.

For some, it's easy to find something to compliment. If you take a look at someone's physical appearance and anything at all stands out, then that's what you should compliment. Whatever the case, beginning to think in terms of positivity toward others will train you to become a better conversationalist. But those are the low-hanging fruit of giving compliments—there are only so many times you can hear that you have nice eyes and still care. How do you give compliments that are more thoughtful and less superficial?

For maximum impact, compliment people for two things (besides the obvious and superficial). Compliment people on (1) things they have control over and (2) things they have made a conscious choice about. There may be significant overlap between the two.

For instance, no one has control over the color of their eyes; thus, it's not a very impactful compliment. However, someone has made a very conscious choice to wear a specific hairstyle that takes an hour to get ready. Other examples include specific habits, specific words and phrases people use, distinct fashion sense, unique thoughts, and so on.

Why are these aspects so much more personal and impactful to compliment?

Because they reflect the person's thought processes and identity. These are choices people consciously make to represent themselves—their tastes and values. They don't do it for others, but they are hoping to be judged positively and lauded for their choices. The more outrageous something might be, the more valuable positive confirmation is. Therefore, when you compliment someone on their choices and thoughts, you validate them to the highest degree.

You can see that complimenting them on something they don't have control over, such as their eye color, doesn't amount to much other than "Hey, congratulations on winning the genetic lottery with your eyes!" Now, if this person was wearing colored contacts, it might be a better compliment because that's obviously a choice they made to alter their original eye color.

Compliment things that they've obviously put some thought into. This might include a bright shirt, a distinctive handbag, an unusual piece of art, or a vintage car. These things are out of the ordinary, uncommon, and reflect a deliberate deviation from the norm. You never know if someone's persona is ingrained in the fact that they choose to wear Hawaiian shirts. By complimenting someone on something they've clearly chosen with purpose, you acknowledge and validate the statement they have chosen to make about themselves.

Other things you can compliment people on that show individual choice are their manners, the way they phrase certain ideas, their opinions, their worldview, and their perspective.

Above all else, compliments trigger one of the most fundamental weaknesses humans have: we are starved for attention. We like to be put in the spotlight and given the attention that we feel we deserve. People aren't really complimented that much on a daily basis—especially men. We can easily see this because most people don't know how to take a true and genuine compliment without a bit of awkward fumbling. Make it a goal to see people fumble about the compliments you give them—that means it impacts them more because they simply don't get many, and it impacts your relationship more.

On a related matter, try to make it a habit to notice, point out, and celebrate people's idiosyncrasies. Everyone has their own sort of either mental, emotional, or physical idiosyncrasy that makes them uniquely *them*, and it can take unlimited forms.

You might think that these idiosyncrasies are things that people want to hide and conceal from others. But here's the surprise: when you notice, point them out, and celebrate them, they'll love you for it.

In the context of conversation, it's going to be things like their mannerisms, tics, gestures, body language, vocabulary, unique phrasing, or even how they cross their legs. There is a multitude of other possibilities.

For instance, everyone has a different physical ritual they engage in, mostly subconsciously, when they speak to others. If it's not a physical ritual during conversation, everyone has different ways they perceive and go about their day. Some people will chew 50 times for each mouthful of food. Others will avoid touching doorknobs when opening doors. And some might avoid stepping on cracks in the sidewalk for fun.

Once you have observed the same idiosyncrasy at least a few times to make sure it's not because of a mosquito or some other environmental factor, draw attention to it! Not in a negative manner, but in an observant manner.

- *Hey, that's an interesting way of tying your shoes...*
- *I see that you keep twisting the jars into patterns. Tell me about that.*
- *Do you favor your left arm? You crack it five times every time we walk inside.*
- *Did you read* Nineteen Eighty-Four *recently? You use the word 'goodplus' a lot...*

You're not calling them out. It's not negative. You're just shining the spotlight on something that is personal to them that they thought people might not notice. But you did notice. The fact that you did will make them feel special because you've apparently paid so much attention to them. To continue with the above examples, what do you imagine the response will be? Very likely pleasant shock and a compulsion to open up and elaborate themselves to you.

Make sure that you don't have any judgmental tone in your voice or body language when you call out an idiosyncrasy. You're coming from a perspective of curiosity rather than "Look at the freak!" This is part one of your charm offensive.

Listening with Intent

In some order, here's what people enjoy about conversations: being entertained or entertaining others through sharing. It's a simplification, but in truth, there aren't many more layers of subtlety.

Think about how you feel after you leave a conversation where you don't share much. You probably felt neglected, suppressed, and like it was a bad conversation because you weren't able to add your thoughts. Now imagine a scenario where you were given all the air space you could use and had a captive audience. You'd come away feeling good because you were able to articulate the subtleties of your thoughts.

Remember that this is a chapter about the charm offensive, which means that this is a feeling you should impart to other people. You know how good it feels to express and explain yourself, so don't rob others of that same feeling.

But to be a good listener, you aren't just giving air space and surrendering your turn to speak. A lot of people think that to be a good listener, you just need to shut up and let the other person talk. While to some extent that's true, there are more parts to the puzzle. That's *passive listening*. To the other person, it can feel as if they are speaking to a wall who nods occasionally.

Active listening is what we're after. It reads like a mouthful, but it's simple in practice. You are listening with the intent and purpose to enhance the conversation in a way that keeps the spotlight on the other person.

Let's say that someone says, "Last weekend I

was skiing but I wasn't really having a good time." Passive listening would consist of you saying "Oh, cool" or "Uh huh" and only acknowledging their statement and staying silent afterward. Active listening, and listening with intent and purpose, would consist of any of the following:

- *"Didn't have a good time...?"* (Repeating the last phrase of a person's statement)
- *"So you went skiing but it wasn't the best time?"* (Rephrasing their statement back to them)
- *"Sounds like you were expecting a fun and active weekend but something was wrong or missing?"* (Sum up their thoughts and position)

Again, you are furthering the conversation while keeping the spotlight on the other person. That's the essence of active listening, and it's more than simply repeating people's words. They are hearing you use their own words in a new sentence, which gives the strong impression that you were listening intently. It appears that you are following their train of thought with interest.

You can listen with intent by following up on any and everything people mention, and a few well-placed questions will make you appear to be a super-listener. Remember that your goal is to demonstrate interest and curiosity in a way that encourages other people to continue speaking.

An extension of listening with intent is the two-second rule.

We know that people speak to feel validation and acceptance. Naturally, the worst thing you can do to someone who has the spotlight is to seize it from them, and we do this in various ways without even realizing it. The biggest way that we seize the spotlight is by not appearing to listen to what they are saying.

Even if you are listening with intent, you may not appear to be doing so outwardly. Interestingly enough, one of the ways we appear to not be listening is by jumping in immediately after they finish speaking, no matter how relevant or revelatory what you say is. This is because of the apparent lack of processing and thinking time.

When someone replies to us immediately without a second of silence, it's natural to assume that they didn't really hear you and were formulating their answer in their head as you finished speaking. Indeed, jumping in right after someone speaks is a milder version of an interruption. It just becomes very clear and apparent that they were just waiting for their turn to speak instead of listening. This is where the two-second rule becomes relevant.

After someone speaks, especially longer, more thoughtful, and more personal statements, pause for two seconds before saying anything. That's it. You pause for two seconds to appear like you are soaking in what they've said and truly acknowledging it before replying to it. When somebody stops talking, they usually look at your face. They're looking for a cue that their words have impacted you. Therefore, during those two seconds, be mindful that your facial expression reflects thought and isn't just a blank stare. Fill the two seconds with whatever verbal utterance you might use to indicate thoughtfulness, such as "interesting…"

All it takes is two seconds. Of course, it has the positive side effect of actually slowing you down and making you think about the message the other person is trying to convey. But the rule is really about making people feel that they matter. You're not making the person you're speaking to feel important if you just jump right in after he or she stops speaking.

If you immediately launch into what you have to say, it will plant seeds of doubt in the back of their minds as to your level of respect for them and the importance you gave to their message. Of course, this rule is about creating a perception, which means you can probably get away with listening less if you make people feel like you're listening with focus and attention. This is the second part of the charm offensive: making people feel like you care and they matter. Giving people the spotlight is an entirely different thing from making sure people know they have the spotlight.

"You can make more friends in two months by

becoming interested in other people than you can in two years by trying to get other people interested in you."—Dale Carnegie

Turn Enemies into Friends

An underrated part of the charm offensive is how it can change people's perceptions of you. You can go from stranger to friend quite quickly, but sometimes it's more important to be able to go from enemy to friend. Indeed, it's tough to fathom working and living in an environment where you have bad blood with people you see every day. Most people will just chalk it up to life and the impossibility of being everyone's best friend—this is true, but there are still strategic tactics you can use to convert people to your side.

The first step, surprisingly, is discovering for the first time in your life who is and is not on your side.

If someone asked you to make a list of all your friends and another list of all your enemies, in theory that's an easy task. But do you know what really makes the difference between those two sets of people in your life? Aside from the obvious fact that there's mutual liking between you and your friends and a mutual dislike between you and your enemies, what else differentiates them?

The answer, according to Dr. Paul Dobransky, is critical advocacy. A friend plays the role of both a constructive critic and an advocate for you, while an enemy is neither—though the enemy may do other things that masquerade as beneficial toward you, they won't be a constructive critic or true advocate for you.

What exactly are critics and advocates in this context? Consider your social interactions and communications as having two aspects: data and emotion. The "data" aspect is addressed by the critic, while the "emotion" aspect is addressed by the advocate.

Critics can be constructive and positive or destructive and malicious, but your friends will only be the positive type. Positive critics have three main qualities: they are concerned, competent, and constructive. They are genuinely concerned about your well-being, know you well enough to be competent at offering an accurate opinion of you, and are constructive in offering suggestions and solutions. In other words, they operate with mature intellect in using information about you and your friendship.

Advocates, on the other hand, are your ever-loyal, optimistic supporters. They radiate positive energy in your life and imbue your relationship with positive emotions. They readily stand by you no matter what. That they're your advocates doesn't necessarily make them your constructive critics, though. Some advocates in your life may not actually be well informed about who you are and are just blindly supporting you even in decisions that are ultimately harmful for you. This is what makes advocacy alone an insufficient quality for friendship. Your friends are those who are both your advocates and your constructive critics, knowing when it's appropriate to counter you from making ill-advised decisions.

Those you consider enemies are neither constructive critics nor advocates in your life. They may instead be destructive or incompetent critics, quick to judge you and your actions without first gathering enough data to make a well-informed opinion about you. Whatever the case, they don't have your best interests in mind.

The great news is that there isn't just one way to turn your enemies into your friends; there are at least three. Suggested by Patrick Allan, these strategies will help you charm your way into making your enemies like you and foster better relationships with them like you never thought possible.

First, stop being the enemy in *their* lives. If you think they're an enemy in your life, don't forget the flipside—that they're thinking of *you* as an enemy in their own lives. How you act toward someone will be reflected back at you in a self-fulfilling prophecy. If you continue indulging their impression of you as an enemy, they'll also continue treating you like one and not tire with antagonizing you every chance they get.

So instead of pushing back with more antagonism, use a little reverse psychology on them and try to get on their side. Be kind and polite toward them, and treat them how they prefer to be treated. Say your supervisor seems to be antagonizing you for no obvious reason (to you). She uses every opportunity to make you feel inferior compared to her. She obviously likes being right and enjoys being seen as the expert, so why not let her win those arguments and praise her superior knowledge and insight? Stop viewing her as the enemy and let her have a win here and there. The time will come when she'll realize you're not challenging her superiority, so she'll feel less need to impose it on you. Admittedly, this step requires willpower.

Secondly, show your enemies that they're surrounded by people who are your allies. In other words, make it known that people like you, you have friends, and, if so many people have a positive impression of you, they surely must be mistaken. You need to show your enemies that the rest of your (and possibly their) social circle finds your company delightful or beneficial in some way. For example, while your antagonistic supervisor is within earshot, express enthusiastic interest in your colleagues' lives or offer to help them in a project they're working on. By power of social influence, eventually your enemies will be swayed into seeing you may not be so bad to have as an ally or a friend, after all. This is the power of perception at work.

Finally, find or create a common enemy. Having a third party you and your "original" enemy have to fight together forces you to work with each other in order to win, or at the very least find common ground to commiserate together. Say your work team is having problems with an unreasonable client. Grab that opportunity to bond with your antagonistic supervisor. Relate to her in such a way that helps her realize "*Hey, we're on the same team now, with someone else who's antagonizing us both.*" She'll be led to think of you as an ally against this common enemy, which will likely help her be more open about knowing you and the strengths you could offer. With that, you'll be slowly converting her into at least a better-informed critic. Who knows? That may then lead her to develop positive emotions toward you (especially if you help her win), turning her into an advocate.

And when she's become your competent critic and positive advocate, you know what that means—she's been converted from your enemy to your friend.

Interrupting to Agree

The final part of your charm offensive arsenal might be unexpected. Most pieces of advice on conversation will advise that you never, ever interrupt others. They'll invariably say that interrupting is rude and sends the wrong message to other people. It's selfish and violates the golden rule of conversation, which is to let others talk about themselves ad nauseum.

There's some truth to that. If you interrupt constantly and don't let people get on track with what they want to say, they will eventually start to hate you because you come off as selfish and self-absorbed. They'll only be able to finish half-thoughts, and that's like stopping a golf club mid-swing continually. You also aren't building the connection you think you are because you are constantly focusing inwardly. This is all to say that interrupting as a *general* rule is not a bad recommendation.

But to not interrupt as an *ironclad* rule is fairly incorrect. The reason interruptions are bad at their core is because they cut off people's trains of thoughts in a negative manner. But what about interrupting in a positive manner to *enhance* someone's train of thought?

Thus, we have this conversation tactic: *the only time you should be interrupting is when you interrupt to agree.* This is something you can wield to build rapport and break down barriers. Interrupt because you are in fact so excited about what someone else is saying that you can't hold it in and have to finish their sentences with them! After your interruption, make sure to digress and let them continue—this time with an injection of enthusiasm from your end.

Similarly, you can interrupt to complete that person's sentence and interrupt to show that you are emotionally aligned with them and on the same page.

- *I was just in Greece and loved it when...*

> [interruption] *No way! That is so exciting and Greece is my favorite place in the whole world!*

- *And then I tried parking there and the meter maid...* [interruption] *Was terrible and ticketed you anyway despite the sign, right?! She's the worst.*
- *That movie was amazing. I just couldn't believe when...* [interruption] *The ending, right?! It was such a shocker and crazy twist!*
- *I couldn't believe it. I absolutely...* [interruption] *Hated that book, right?! I totally agree!*

With each of these interruptions, make sure to take a step back and don't steal their thunder and run on your own tangent. Just interrupt to show matching levels of emotion, and let them continue.

The examples above all denote a level of excitement for what the other person is talking about. So you are interrupting with a purpose and not just blindly to interject something randomly about yourself. You are interrupting to agree, commiserate, show your emotional engagement, and *feel* together. You are also interrupting because you feel as strongly about the subject as they do. You have the same level of emotional urgency, and that is key. Instead of challenging them, you are agreeing heavily, and who doesn't like to be agreed with?

If you can predict the emotional direction someone is taking and want to inject a sentiment of agreement, interrupt to agree. Just make sure you don't guess wrong and say the opposite of their sentiment.

For example: *I know! It's so...*

And then you allow them to finish the statement with *"amazing!"* or *"horrible!"* so you can see which direction they are going. When you speak in unison with somebody, this creates emotional unison.

As annoying twins often say, they are so close that they can finish each other's sentences. What they might not realize is that it works the opposite way as well—if you can finish each other's sentences, then you can create the feeling of familiarity and closeness.

Takeaways:

- Whatever the reason, sometimes we find ourselves in a position where we *really* want to make a good impression. Normal conversation tactics to build rapport won't do here. What can really move the needle?
- Obviously, the first way to charm people is to pay them compliments early and often. But there are specific compliments that really impact the recipients. You should seek to compliment people on things they have made a conscious choice about and that reflect their thinking process. This gives them validation in a way that complimenting them on their eyes simply doesn't.
- The charm offensive is powerful because it allows you to change people's perceptions of you. There is a process of converting an enemy to a friend, and it involves changing your own perception, invoking social proof, and creating or finding a common enemy.
- Finally, we've always learned that we shouldn't interrupt people. Normally, we

shouldn't, but you have full permission to interrupt to agree and emphasize a shared emotion.

Chapter 5. Slipping Away and Out

Now this is a chapter that is plainly and obviously valuable. How can we slip away from people, whether you're sick of them, they never stop talking, or you just want to go to the bathroom? It's usually a touchy topic, which is why we tend to allow people to talk our ears off, in the desperate hope that they can see our nonverbal cues.

Here's a tip: they won't. Even if they do, they don't care and are more interested in hearing the sound of their voice, whether intentionally or not. Whatever the case, you've been reduced to nodding and saying "Uh huh" for the past 20 minutes with no end in sight. What do you do?

The reason it's tough for us to directly and straightforwardly either leave a conversation or interrupt someone is because we know what it feels like ourselves. We know the gut-punch feeling when someone turns away from us while we are mid-sentence or makes a generic excuse to walk away. We want to keep others from those feelings as well, and so we don't feel comfortable saying anything directly.

We try to rely on indirect cues such as "I have to be going soon..." or slowly giving one-word answers in the hopes that they will grow bored and find other prey. It's the conversational equivalent of playing possum, and it almost never works.

The Psychology of Leaving

The lights are dimmed down, the music's up, the drinks are flowing, and the room's abuzz with chatter and laughter. This party is rockin'.

But you want to leave. Maybe you're an introvert who just doesn't have the energy to socialize for as long as your other extraverted friends do. Maybe you've got somewhere else you need to be. Or maybe you just really need to get home because you've got work to do or you've got a big thing coming up the next morning and you want to get a good night's rest.

All these are perfectly valid reasons to leave the party—just as important of a scenario as getting away from someone that won't stop talking. But something's stopping you from leaving. It may be the fact that no one else has left the party, which you take as a sign that it's still too early to leave without offending the host. Or maybe you're dreading having to explain your early departure to the host and to the other guests. The thought of rambling about, dishing your excuses and apologetic smiles left and right as you try to exit the scene, is enough to dissuade you from actually leaving. And so you stay. You're no longer enjoying yourself, but you stay because you don't want to have to say goodbye.

If this distressing scenario sounds familiar to you, there's a simple remedy to your woes the next time you're in a similar situation. When you're at a party and want to leave but don't want to say goodbye, just do exactly that. Leave without saying goodbye.

Known as the "Irish goodbye," this strategy involves simply slipping away in silence while the party is going on. Just grab your coat and make your way out. Also known as "ghosting," the "French exit," or the "low profile exit," the Irish goodbye may seem rude on the surface, but deeper consideration of the psychology behind it and its effects reveals that it's actually a form of politeness. How so?

See, the intent behind the Irish goodbye isn't snobbery but subtlety. Take a moment to consider how announced goodbyes at parties really go. You writhe in discomfort for at least half an hour, trying to debate with yourself whether you should stay or just go. Once you decide to leave, you practice what you're going to say in your head, then inch your way toward the hosts. You wait for them to break free from whatever social circle they're currently entangled in. When you finally get to talk to them, you inform them that you're leaving, which then commences the formulaic back-and-forth:

"Oh no, but why?"
[Insert your reason/excuse here]
"But the night's still young!"
[You restate your reason/excuse and insist you have to leave]
"Look, I still need to introduce you to so and so..." [This is where the hosts bring up other fun stuff set to occur later in the party]

And so it continues, until one of you buckles to the pressure and the goodbye conversation eventually dwindles down to awkward small talk as you both try to find a point at which you could comfortably end the conversation and go your separate ways again.

Now imagine the hosts having to go through this sort of interaction several times over for the same number of guests they had invited to their party. They'll end up spending the last half of the celebration entertaining the people who're leaving instead of enjoying the company of those who're staying. The other guests who witness your big farewell will also be likely to stop whatever they're doing just to say goodbye to you, thus shifting the focus from celebration to send-off.

So the next time you're leaving a party halfway through, just gather your coat, choose an exit route that won't draw much attention, and silently head out. You'll be saving the hosts and guests from having to pause the celebratory mood, and you'll also be saving yourself the trouble of navigating through explanations and awkward goodbyes.

The only downside of the Irish goodbye is the possibility of the hosts interpreting it as a sign that you didn't enjoy the party, so counter this by shooting them a text or an email immediately afterward. Thank them for inviting you and highlight specific things in the party you especially enjoyed (*"The DJ's mix was amazing; can you gel me his contact details? I want to keep it on file for the next time I throw a party"*).

Another way to classily pull an Irish goodbye is to execute a "smooth exit" by informing your hosts about it ahead of time. Upon arriving and greeting them, tell them you're going to have to leave early but you're looking forward to having a good time while you're there. You may also request someone at the party to inform the others of your leave-taking on your behalf, should anyone ask. And of course, don't forget to send your hosts a message of thanks and word that you had a great time.

Remember, though, that the Irish goodbye is ideal only for larger gatherings (more than 15 people). If there are fewer attendees, slipping away is less likely to be seen as polite consideration and more likely to be considered ditching, so better let the group know you're leaving when attendees number fewer than 15. Also, opt for announcing your goodbye to everyone (or at least to the host) when the party is for you or for an immediate relative or when the event is a formal one (think sit-down dinners with place cards).

So when you do need to let people know you're leaving, just how do you transition from happily chatting away with the group to taking leave without ending things on a sorry note? Marlen Komar suggests making your final spiel a witty, funny short story. As you near telling the end of it, stand up, grab your stuff, hug the host, and deliver your punchline. While everyone's laughing, thank them for the great evening and make your way out. This would assure everyone that you've had a great time and are not leaving because you find the company boring.

Not much of an animated storyteller but want to leave without having everyone think you hated the party or left in low spirits? Avoid watching the clock and instead project an aura of energy and enthusiasm. In the moments right before you leave, make it look like you're having the time of your life, enjoying the band's music and cracking jokes. That way, when you do leave, people won't think it's because the party was a letdown or because you're a recluse just tolerating the festivities. You might even have them secretly suspecting you have to leave because there's another bash you'll attend after you've stepped out the door.

Another way to exit graciously is to catch the host while he or she is in a relatively less crowded area (e.g., the kitchen, the hallway, or the porch) and discreetly bid him or her goodbye there. This is way better than announcing your adieu while your host is smack in the middle of the crowd, entertaining guests left and right. By saying your goodbye while your host is by himself as he refills the ice bucket, or by herself as she makes her way from one hub to another, you'll be less likely to disrupt the celebratory atmosphere of the party—and you'll also have fewer people pressuring you to stay.

There are also times when it's the hosts themselves who hint that they're ready for people to start leaving. They may do this by constantly checking on their watches, getting a major cleanup going on, stopping the music and bringing on the lights, or strategically transferring guests' coats from the back room to a sofa arm. Be sensitive to these signs to avoid overstaying your welcome.

Once you gather that your hosts are ready to say goodbye, approach them and maybe offer to help clean up. They're likely to decline your offer, especially if you're not a relative or very close friend, in which case thank them for a wonderful time and bid them farewell. If the crowd's still large enough and you see that your hosts are too busy to entertain any more interruptions, then simply pull the Irish goodbye and send them a thank-you message afterward. You'll be doing them—and yourself—a favor.

The Great Escape

Now for the arguably more valuable application of slipping away and out: when you just don't care who you're with or what they're talking about. You want to leave an interaction and hopefully not insult the people you are with in the process. You never know when a goodbye will turn into a 10-minute conversation—this is why many of us actually avoid goodbyes.

But if that's how you leave or disengage, you can come off as hostile or socially incompetent. You have to master the art of *bowing out of conversations* gracefully and heading for the exit. Here are five useful excuses and how to make sure they don't sound like excuses.

The call. You can tell others you got a call, text, or email that you need to deal with in some way. Not even your close friends or coworkers know the details of your daily obligations and work duties, so it's easy to simply look at your phone and express surprise or concern—the key is how important the matter seems to be. Almost no one will have a problem with it because they know that urgent issues pop up all the time. It's perfectly legitimate.

"Excuse me, do you mind if I step out and take this?"
"Sorry, I just got something that looks urgent. Do you mind if I head home to take care of this?"

You can also just glance at your phone to see the time and say something like "Wow, I didn't realize the time. Do you mind if we continue this later? [insert something that sounds urgent but others have no way of verifying.]"

You don't even have to elaborate much on what you are supposedly dealing with, and people will rarely ask.

Another subtlety is to ask for permission to be excused. It's a gesture of goodwill. It makes it clear that you are taking the other person into consideration and being courteous so as to not reject them for something else. Besides, it's not like anyone will refuse permission by saying, "No, stay here and talk. I'm more important than your job."

The bathroom. Second, you can tell others you need to be excused to use the bathroom. Just make this excuse seem urgent, and they'll completely understand it. Again, this is because literally everyone has felt the sting of the growing water balloon inside them when they have to resist going to the bathroom. "Wait, I'm sorry. I've been squeezing my bladder ever since I got here and I've got stomach cramps now. Can you excuse me?"

Another person. Third, similarly to the bathroom scenario, you can say you need to talk to someone else. This may seem like it would be rude, but people have no problem with this if you do it correctly. The key is to make it seem important and urgent.

If you see someone walking by, you could say, "Oh wait, is that Steve? I'm sorry. I need to catch him, and I've been calling him constantly. Can you excuse me?"

If you're isolated and you don't see anyone walking by, you could say, "I know this is random, but do you think Steve is around? I called him three times and he didn't get back to me. I think I need to check on him. Can you excuse me?"

Pawn. This is when you pawn the person you are talking to off to a friend or someone that is walking by. There are a few steps to this.

First, look around and see who you can pawn this person off to. Second, try to catch the attention of the other person so they will come your direction. You can also slowly walk your way over to the new person. If you are talking to someone who won't shut up, they will follow you step by step.

Third, when you make contact, introduce the two people to each other. The key to this tactic is to make each person sound incredibly fascinating so they will immediately engage with each other. Introduce each person with one or two of their most interesting traits or experiences, and this should be easy. You're putting yourself in the periphery of the interaction and making the new people the focuses.

"Oh hey, this is Barry. Barry is our resident karaoke master and runs marathons. Michelle had a pig as a pet when she was a child and drinks about four Diet Cokes a day."

Now that the focus is off you, there is less pressure for you to escape gracefully. All you need to do make a small excuse, like any of the excuses in this chapter, and walk away. You may not even need to say anything if your captor is excited by this new person.

The four tactics in leaving I mentioned have a few themes in common, which is why I also want to provide a small framework for the most acceptable way to escape an interaction. If you find yourself in a situation where you can invoke all of these factors, you can escape anything without ruffling feathers.

First, have an excuse ready to leave any conversation or social situation. The bathroom, needing to call someone, or searching for someone else always work. It doesn't have to be too specific; just have something ready on the tip of your tongue.

Second, act as if the need for an exit is urgent so the other people in your context won't take it personally or question it. This is important because we sometimes feel that leaving a conversation is tantamount to rejecting someone. In a way, it is, but we can mask that feeling by conveying urgency and importance. No one is going to feel insulted if you need to go home because your apartment is flooding. Urgency eliminates bruised feelings.

Third, ask for permission and then apologize for having to leave. Drive home how genuine and courteous you are. Show remorse about the fact that you are escaping and they'll feel good about it. How nice is the person who asks for permission to go home and deal with a flooded apartment? Amazing!

Finally, say something about continuing in the near future to cap off your regret at having to leave. For example, "Let's do this again soon" or "I want to continue this conversation!" This adds a final level of empathy and care so people can feel good about the fact that you are departing but not wishing to.

As you can see, most of these factors are aimed toward obscuring the fact that you simply don't want to be there anymore and sparing the feelings of the other people. You are conveying your full message, but without the negative impact.

These four steps can help you build an exit strategy for wherever you go and whatever situation you find yourself in. Is it deceptive? Some could see it that way, but if the alternative is to get cornered by someone who lacks the self-awareness to see you yawning while you are already exhausted, making you grumpy and annoyed, then I would choose to convey the message without the impact every time.

Takeaways:

- This may not be the most important skill overall, but it's the most important skill for your sanity. How can we get away from people but in a graceful manner?
- There are many types of goodbyes and ways to leave. They are separate: leaving an event or party is not necessarily the same as leaving an interaction. As for leaving an event or party, the Irish Goodbye is particularly effective because it is actually a gesture of kindness for everyone involved. Otherwise, you can isolate your host, leave on a high note, or simply set expectations ahead of time so you feel less guilt about slipping away.
- Besides those, there are certain methods of getting away from interactions and people gracefully: the call, the bathroom, introductions, and using other people as pawns. These all share a few common elements to make these moves socially acceptable and subtle: having an excuse, creating urgency, asking for permission, and mentioning the future.

Chapter 6. Specific [Awkward] Situations

Imagine spending about 10 minutes saying goodbye to an acquaintance, departing, and suddenly realizing that you have to walk in the same direction for five blocks. Does that sound awkward to you? What about commenting on someone's weight gain, only to learn that they're pregnant?

These aren't infrequent situations we get ourselves into. Daily life is fraught with potential awkward circumstances, and it's more impressive if you can go a few hours without experiencing one. Despite their frequency, you may or may not have gotten better at handling these situations. That's what this chapter is for. If some of our daily conversations have awkward elements in them, then it's about time to learn tactics to deal with them.

The first step is to understand briefly *why* awkward moments occur. What creates that feeling of discomfort and *"I have no idea how to handle myself at this moment."*

To answer this, I propose a compelling reason for awkward moments: they happen because all of the parties involved don't know what to do simultaneously. Usually in a conversation or interaction, one party takes charge, or at the very least, there is a social script that people can conform to. They generally have an idea of what to do, how to act, what to say, what not to say, and how to resolve the situation.

For instance, suppose you have a relatively good friend you haven't seen for a while. Do you go for a handshake, a hug, or, if you're European, a kiss on the cheek? There's no set script here, so people are left to their own devices to figure out how to act. This, of course, leaves you in the midst of an awkward mess. But now take the setting of a formal restaurant—you have an idea of how you should act because you have gradually learned the script for that situation.

When parties are at a loss for how to act, there is hesitation and a general sense of fumbling around until the situation resolves itself naturally. Another example: an awkward situation is like cars merging in traffic without clear traffic laws. Without an understanding of how the traffic should merge, there is tension, discomfort, and an occasional crash. This is all eliminated when someone takes charge and creates a script for people to follow. Therefore, most of these situations are solved by someone blasting through the ambiguity and taking the lead. If there's no script, someone can set a script, and that someone should be you.

Can simply taking charge of the situation and acting first obliterate all awkward situations? Of course not. That's what the rest of this chapter is for. But setting a tone for people to follow would certainly help with the earlier example of the kiss/handshake/hug debacle if you were to clearly open your arms and motion for a hug. The uncomfortable ambiguity in who should do what when would be alleviated.

So let's dive into a few of those awkward situations and how to handle them with less scrambling and fewer sweaty palms.

What's Your Name, Again?

You know his face and you even know where he works. But his name eludes your memory at the moment. Uh-oh, how do you deal with this and covertly learn his name without letting him feel unmemorable and unimportant? This is another instance where we don't want to make others feel small and awkward.

Has this happened to you before? Then you know it feels borderline insulting to be asked your name after meeting them once or twice before. It truly gives the impression they don't care about you and you aren't memorable—maybe you weren't to them, but at least they can keep that under wraps.

What are some ways to sneakily discover someone's name without having to ask them for it directly? The most obvious way is to sneak away and ask someone else in the vicinity, but this isn't always possible and there aren't always other people around. Therefore, these methods involve getting the person to say their name for another purpose than to tell you.

Think of it like the fairy tale of *Rumpelstiltskin*. In this fairy tale, a creature named Rumpelstiltskin will only give relief to a family if the family can guess his name, which is difficult to say the least. The family sends a messenger to communicate with this beast, and in the process, the messenger observes Rumpelstiltskin talking out loud to himself in the third person and revealing his name when he thought no one was around. The story typically ends with Rumpelstiltskin becoming so angry that he inadvertently tears himself in two. Ignoring the end of the story, we can apply some of these lessons.

First, you can introduce this mystery person to a friend or anyone else nearby. It's not necessary to know the names of either people. You can just grab both people and say, "Hey, have you two met each other?" and they will naturally introduce themselves with their names and shake hands. Of course it helps if the person nearby is a friend of yours. "This is my friend Bob" and Bob will immediately ask for the mystery person's name. Then you can chime in.

Second, you can ask them for their contact information or business card. Make clear that it's for the purpose of wanting to keep in touch in the future. If they want to give you their phone number, insist they enter it into your phone so they actually have to type their name in first. If they want to give you their email address, often their name will be in it. Ideally, they give you a business card so you have their full name to refer to.

If attaining their contact information somehow doesn't bring up their name, you can ask them to spell their name for you by claiming that you are terrible with spelling. Even if their name is common like Kevin or Eric, you can still claim that you recently met someone who spelled their name "Keavan" or "Eryck" so you just need to make sure!

Finally, you can always apologize and claim

to be a combination of terrible with names and stressed out on the day you met originally. This is probably the answer closest to the honest answer of "I didn't pay enough attention to you so I forgot." Most people have had days like this, so there is some level of understanding if you emphasize how bad of a day it was for you.

On the flip side, what about when people don't appear to remember your name? There are two ways of dealing with this, and most people choose the one that inadvertently creates tension.

Bad and tense: "Hey, you don't remember my name, do you?" This instantly puts people on the defensive and is a bit passive-aggressive. It makes an assumption and the immediate response to this will be an apology. Why start a conversation off with that tone?

Better: "Hey, I'm Bob. We met at Ned's party. I'm not sure if you recall. How are you doing?" This takes charge and allows the other person to save face and skip the discomfort of not knowing. Not remembering someone's name can be embarrassing, but it's a condition that is easily fixable. Remember, taking charge and creating a script for people to follow is what obliterates awkwardness.

Accepting Compliments

We give compliments on a fairly frequent basis, but why exactly do we give them? You might be paying a compliment as part of your charm offensive or simply be thinking out loud about an observation about someone.

Whatever the case, the end effect is that people feel better about themselves and more positively about you. We're after the positive consequences of a compliment—they feel better about themselves, and that translates to the conversation and their feelings about you. Giving a compliment is easy, and we've even covered some ways to make them special. But in practice, *accepting and receiving* compliments is rarely a smooth process. Some people know what to say, but most fumble with it.

Think back to the last compliment you paid someone. You may imagine that it sends people to cloud nine, but the path was probably a bit more twisted. What happened after it was given?

Most people, including you, often don't know how to handle direct praise and become uncomfortable when confronted with it. We live in societies that are both passive and hateful of pride, so this shouldn't be a surprise. When we avoid being direct in our lives, we have no idea what to do when we're face-to-face with it. The response was probably one of the following:

- False modesty—*Oh, my muscles? I didn't know you could see them bulging in this shirt.*
- Awkward stuttering—*Um... you mean my biceps? Thanks... I guess... Um...*
- Flat-out denial masking happiness or belying deep insecurity—*What are you talking about? I'm fat, ugly, and out of shape. You're blind.*
- Direct evocation of a deep insecurity—*I'm fit? I don't know, I used to be the fat kid and I never really see myself as attractive or deserving of anyone...*
- Gratitude then immediately switching

> topics out of discomfort—*Hey, thanks! Um… how about the weather?*

You'll probably recognize each of these responses, and hopefully you can see how each is not ideal. Only the last example doesn't derail a conversation and make both parties feel uncomfortable about being positive. Handling a compliment poorly can stall an interaction.

Sometimes there is a resistance to accepting a compliment because people don't want to be caught in a false positive. In other words, people don't want to genuinely say thank you only to be told someone was kidding or being sarcastic about the compliment. It's the equivalent of waving at someone, only to discover that they weren't waving at you but actually at someone behind you.

So how do you take a compliment gracefully and within the flow of a conversation? You already know that you can accept it directly, but chances are you're not doing that because of the aforementioned fear of a false positive, or plain discomfort showing *pride in yourself.*

Therefore, you can safely accept a compliment by *complimenting the compliment*. This keeps a conversation flowing and also caters to your compulsion to move the attention off of you.

Patrick, your haircut makes you look like a Gap model. *Thanks, when did you get so great at complimenting and flattering people?*

Patrick, the way you shot that gun was nothing short of amazing. *Thanks, you're the one that taught me how to do it, all credit to you.*

Patrick, those are some sweet shoes. *Thanks, you are the most observant person I know.*

Patrick, you have the body of a modern Adonis. *Thanks, you have the funniest comparisons out of anyone I know.*

Complimenting the compliment is more than taking the focus off of you. It allows you to avoid what happens when you either reject or accept a compliment—both of which can have negative consequences.

For example, if I were to agree that my haircut *does* make me look handsome like James Dean, it can be seen as a bit arrogant, can't it? If I were to deny it, it's a bit frustrating for the complimenter and makes me seem like I'm fishing for attention. And so on. You avoid all of the pitfalls that I illustrated in my earlier examples—the pitfalls that stall conversation.

Complimenting the complimenting allows you to deflect your attention onto something else entirely, which lets you bypass talking about the compliment, typically the most uncomfortable part about it. It also injects another positive element into your conversation. Instead of ambiguity and potential awkwardness and negativity, you created a mutual positive situation. This triggers positive reciprocal action. In other words, you share the spotlight and turn a simple compliment into a win-win situation. Compliments are meant to be good, so compliment it back, share the goodness, and welcome more positivity into your life.

Breaking the Ice

Another extremely common awkward situation to prepare for is the act of breaking the ice with a stranger, acquaintance, or even friend. It's not that we don't know what to say—just like with when we forget someone's name, we know the most direct path to getting what we want. The easiest and most direct way of breaking the ice is to just say hello and introduce your name—we just feel supremely uncomfortable using it. Thus arises the need for sly tactics to accomplish what we want through indirect means.

This happens for a multitude of reasons, summed up by the feeling that we are interrupting people or otherwise inconveniencing them. That's one of way looking at it—unfortunately, it's the most common. We have trouble breaking the ice with people, even though it's such a simple thing, because we create a "they'll think" feedback loop in our brains.

For instance, if we suddenly chat up a stranger or barge into two people already having a conversation, we are afraid:

- They'll think I'm a weirdo.
- They'll think I'm a creep.
- They'll think I'm rude.

It doesn't matter that these aren't true—we *think* they are true, and thus they stop us from easy solutions to the problem of breaking the ice. It's a matter of finding a way to deal with this potentially awkward situation and getting ahead of the judgments and assumptions you create for yourself.

How can you feel okay about breaking the ice? By doing it indirectly. In other words, having some sort of excuse or justification to speak to someone—when we have come up with a reason, suddenly it's easy to interrupt people or walk up to a stranger.

For instance, would you have a problem walking up to someone and asking for directions if you were utterly lost and on the verge of exhaustion? Doubtful, and not just because of necessity. You'd feel that you have a compelling reason to speak, and that would override your fear of judgment. That's the meaning of indirect in this context: you have an actual reason to approach someone, and when we can create one for ourselves, we can convince ourselves to take action more easily. In other instances, you might refer to this feeling as the feeling of *plausible deniability*—where you have a plausible reason to walk up and start a conversation in a way that no one can think you're rude or weird.

Therefore, I want to present three indirect methods of breaking the ice that make you feel safe because you aren't necessarily walking up to someone just for the sake of starting a conversation. The biggest part of the battle is making breaking the ice feel acceptable—it's an "I don't feel confident or comfortable" issue more than an "I don't know what to say" issue. Recall that asking for directions on the verge of exhaustion makes all of those worries secondary.

The first, indirect method of breaking the ice is to ask people for *objective information* or a *subjective opinion*. These can be very legitimate and important questions that would necessitate speaking to a stranger. It doesn't necessarily matter that the person you are asking knows the answer; it's just a way to begin a dialogue. For that matter, it doesn't even matter that you *don't* know the answer.

- Excuse me, do you know what time the speeches begin?
- Do you know where the closest Starbucks is?
- What did you think of the CEO's speech?
- Do you like the food here?

The first two examples are asking for objective information, while the latter two are asking for a subjective opinion.

The second, indirect method of breaking the ice is to comment on something in the environment, context, or specific situation. It can be as simple as an observation. Imagine you are thinking out loud and prompting people to answer.

- Did you see that piece of art on the wall? What a crazy concept.
- The lighting in here is beautiful. I think it's worth more than my house.

- This is an amazing DJ. All the rock ballads of the '80s.

Notice how these are all statements and not direct questions. You are inviting someone to comment on your statement instead of asking them to engage.

The third and final indirect method of breaking the ice is to comment on a commonality you both share. For instance, why are you both at your friend Jack's apartment? What business brings you to both to this networking conference in Tallahassee? What stroke of misfortune brought you to the DMV this morning?

- So who do you know here?
- So how do you know Jack?
- Has Jack told you about the time he went skiing with his dog?

The idea with these commonalities is that they are instant topics of conversation because there will be a clear answer behind them. These indirect icebreakers aren't rocket science, but their main value is to make you feel okay with breaking the ice, which is the real problem.

Dealing with Interruptions

A final awkward situation to be ready for on a daily basis is dealing with interruptions. Actually, this goes beyond awkward and straight into the *infuriating category*.

You're explaining the mechanics of how to apply for a research grant to your coworkers. One of them cuts in on you to comment on the tediousness of the process. You allow a few minutes for her rants. Then, when she pauses to take a breath, you thank her for sharing her thoughts and continue. You don't get past your second sentence when she interrupts again to ask a question. You indulge her curiosity and answer, then continue with the process you're trying to explain.

Then she interrupts you again.

If this is a familiar situation for you, you understand how exasperating it can be to try to manage such interruptions without seeming like you're shutting somebody out.

You want your listeners have opinions about what you're discussing, and you don't want to dampen the interactive atmosphere in the room by snubbing those who offer theirs. So how do you deal with intrusive interruptions without sounding like an oppressive authoritarian?

Use the preemptive strike. Suggested by Harvard professor Francesca Gino, this tactic involves explaining beforehand when interruptions will be welcome. For example, you may kick off your presentation by saying, *"There are five main points I want to run down with you so that everyone's oriented on the issue first. Then we'll be soliciting opinions and questions from the group based on what you hear from that."* This lets your listeners know that offering their opinions or questions before you've finished all five points is likely to be premature, so they'll be better off reserving those until the end of the presentation.

If someone still interrupts you during your presentation, you could reinforce the message by saying, *"Allow me to finish giving all five points first like I mentioned Then I want your thoughts.*" This lets your listeners know that it's not that you don't care about what they have to say; it's just that there's a better time to hear them out. When they understand that they'll later have their time to step on the podium and be heard with undivided attention, they'll be less likely to intrude while you're delivering what you have to say.

There may still be times, though, when the preemptive strike is not enough to strike down a constant interrupter. As explained by licensed clinical psychologist Dr. Joel Minden, interrupting during social situations is a way to demonstrate power. Not wanting to surrender that power, some people may insist on dominating conversations by frequent, intrusive interruptions. This differs from the way a friend's excited talk may overlap with yours as you both engage in a lively conversation—that's no biggie. Aggressive interrupters are destructive, butting in constantly to demonstrate their power.

To deal with frequent, intrusive interrupters, writer Rose Eveleth suggests calling the other person out on their intrusion, repeating their name over and over, and interrupting back until they finally give way to you. However, Dr. Minden points out that this may lead to a power battle that you're unlikely to win if you're not the confrontational type.

Nonetheless, Dr. Minden says that effectively dealing with constant interrupters will still call for a degree of assertiveness. You'll need to learn how to hold your own conversational ground. If you feel intimidated by the idea of asserting your own right to talk uninterrupted, consider changing the way you think about assertiveness. It's not about being confrontational; it's about being open and direct about what you think is the appropriate way to hold a productive conversation.

Say your colleague insists on interrupting you with irrelevant comments during your presentation. You may deal with the situation by saying, "*I'd appreciate it if you reserve your comments and questions for the end of the presentation. I'd like to finish discussing these points first so we could make the best use of the time we have."*

Now what about in situations when it's you who's accidentally interrupted someone or you're witnessing another speaker being interrupted? How do you reel the conversation back to a place where the person interrupted doesn't feel like they're being disregarded?

Simple. Immediately after the interruption, ask that person to continue. Say that as you hasten to elaborate on a point your colleague has raised, you accidentally talk over him and draw the attention of the room to your explanation instead. Once you realize what has happened, address your interrupted colleague with "*You raised a great point about the advantage of tapping local community resources. May we hear the rest of what you intended to say about it?*" This will let your colleague, as well as the rest of the group, know that you heard his point clearly and are interested in the complete expression of his views about it.

The world will never run out of interruptions

to riddle your day with, but the mission is not to eliminate them entirely—it's to learn how to handle them effectively.

Takeaways:

- Awkward situations occur just about every day, yet they are still awkward because we never learn how to deal with them. So how do you deal with awkward? By taking charge and setting the tone and eliminating the ambiguity that causes the awkward in the first place.
- But it's also helpful to provide blueprints on how to deal with common awkward situations you might come across. The first is forgetting someone else's name, and that's a matter of getting them to say their name without you directly asking. You can introduce them to someone else, ask for their contact info, ask them to spell their last name, or just fess up that you forgot and it's not personal.
- Accepting compliments is also something people handle with discomfort, and it's just a matter of deflecting the attention from yourself and complimenting the compliment. In this way, you can turn

positivity one way into positivity for two people.
- Breaking the ice with strangers is never a comfortable feeling, but that's because it feels intrusive and rude. If you can give yourself a plausible reason for speaking to people, then you can easily interject and break the ice. For instance, you can ask for information or an opinion. You can also comment on something that is shared or comment on something in the environment.
- Finally, dealing with interruptions can save your sanity because interruptions are frustrating. You can use a preemptive strike to let people know that you don't want to be interrupted. You can continually emphasize it and use it as a barometer to gauge who will respect your space. If you are the one who interrupts, then make it a habit to bring things back to what the other person was saying.

Chapter 7. Stop, Please

Suppose you climbed Mount Everest as a child. Or that you once resurrected a lamb by giving it mouth to mouth resuscitation for over an hour. Or perhaps you were the inspiration for the Harry Potter books because of your wild imagination and fascination with riding brooms. You'd imagine that people would be clamoring to speak to you and listen to your stories.

You could be the most interesting person in the world, but no one will care if you engage in conversational habits that, for lack of a better word, repulse people. Indeed, as you might have seen in your daily life, sometimes it's an overall net gain if you don't have to deal with people that annoy the heck out of you, no matter how much of a benefit they represent. It's not a stretch to propose that you'd highly prefer someone that was milquetoast yet not annoying or frustrating.

In other words, appearing benign and non-annoying will probably make you a better conversationalist than being someone who is actually interesting but has frustrating interpersonal habits. Thankfully, we have learned a multitude of conversation tactics to make you appealing and captivating—now let's make sure you're not exhibiting toxic habits and behaviors.

The first step is evaluating how people act around you. This is to diagnose whether you are indeed repulsing people. The art of gaining self-awareness is difficult, but we can take a shortcut here. Instead of shining a flashlight onto ourselves, we can evaluate how the people around you receive you. In that way, it's like measuring an object's gravity to find its mass. You can figure out if you have any toxic habits just by seeing your push on people around you.

For instance, are you creating anxiety or stress in people? If so, they won't perform well around you, they'll avoid eye contact, and they'll hide details of their lives because they fear you'll judge them. They'll also stay out of your way and willingly let you make mistakes. This is all done so they don't invoke your wrath.

Do people ask you questions? If they tend to give you one-word answers or not ask about you, it means they are either not interested or uncomfortable engaging with you. An easy way to cope with that discomfort is to simply avoid. You can also tell if there is a group consensus because the entire group suddenly falls quiet when you walk into the room. Why? Because they were talking about you. If you feel like people end conversations prematurely with you, they might actually be doing so.

Sometimes people *let* awkward silences form to discourage further interaction. A pause is not always an invitation for you to fill the silence.

When people suddenly get extremely general

in the topics they introduce, especially in regard to future plans, it's a sign they want to wind the conversation down and move on. For example, "What are you doing the rest of the day?" or "What do you have planned for the weekend?" are typically cues for wanting to disengage and move on with their day.

What could be causing these negative reactions?

You Only See Black and White

Put another way, you only see one correct way of doing things, and anything that diverges from that view is wrong. And that way happens to be your view.

This habit is particularly toxic because people who have this mindset are judgmental. When they come across people who don't fit the mold of how they feel the world should operate, they judge them, sometimes to their faces. They are prone to thinking of that person as someone who is wrong and can only respond in a very stereotypical way. You might think you're open-minded, but if you only have criticisms and judgments of others, you're probably not.

Just as you wouldn't want to be put in a box the moment you talk to people, others also don't respond all that well to feeling as if they're being judged. This is a hard habit to break because opinions can easily become personal. When you act this way, you tend to offend people and make them feel like they can't express themselves around you.

If somebody has an opinion, respect that opinion. Ask questions about how they came up with that opinion and what information and assumptions they hold.

Give people the benefit of the doubt. At least assume they have reasonable underpinnings for their opinions and beliefs. What experiences have they had in their lives that might explain why they hold a position in such contrast to yours? Remember that people have their own reasons for opinions and beliefs and that not everybody thinks just the way you do. You can either recognize this or not.

In other words, you are a full-fledged, card-carrying, badge-wearing member of the *Belief Police*.

This causes us to spend way too much time squabbling over things just because we feel that other people believe or think something different than we do and must be corrected. If we're honest, it's because our ego feels a little bit bruised so we feel the need to inflict that same feeling on others.

If you've ever been around a know-it-all, you know exactly what I'm talking about. If you don't, you might be a member of the Belief Police. *Open the door! You're wrong about something!*

A Belief Policeman might be very effective at imposing their beliefs on others, but this habit is going to make you downright obnoxious to talk to, and not in an affectionately obnoxious kid sister kind of way. Who wants to spend time with someone who makes them feel judged, attacked, and defensive? So people stop opening up to you and will eventually avoid you altogether. Eventually, they'll just avoid you so they can avoid the feeling of having to censor themselves.

Everything is an opportunity to show just how vastly superior your knowledge and experience are compared to the person you are conversing with. But at what cost does this come? And in the end, does it really matter?

This is especially true when it comes to matters of taste and opinion. These are completely subjective. What looks good to you might be completely ugly to another person. You won't convince anyone to like chocolate more than they already do or to like beets when they hate them, so it's really a waste of your time—and an extremely annoying one at that—to exert your energy trying to convince them.

Just let others be right (or think they are right) most of the time. Choose your battles and don't fret about the small details of what you can't change. You'll be happier and less stressed, and you'll notice a direct correlation between that and the quality of your friendships and interactions.

You Give Unsolicited Thoughts

Many times, people just want to talk about something and think out loud. They're not looking to debate, realize something profound, hear advice, or act on anything. They just want to be heard and validated in a comfortable setting. In many cases, they just want to get a weight off of their chest and share feelings. In fact, they want to hear their own voices. This doesn't mean they are conversational narcissists; they are simply having an internal monologue externally.

You might know where I'm heading with this. Sometimes you just need a sounding board or a shoulder to cry or whine on. You need someone to say, "Oh, that sucks!"

And that's it. For a lot of us, that's all we're looking for. You can also think of this as validation—in this context, it's essentially where you make someone feel good about what they feel. You take their emotion and make them feel justified and comfortable with them. You don't necessarily have to agree with them; you are just acknowledging them. It's not about you at all—keep the focus on them.

You have probably used these if you have ever had to listen to a friend rant about a coworker or a significant other. It sounds like this:

- That must have been terrible.
- I can't even imagine how you must have felt.
- It seems like you have good reason to be angry.
- It is ridiculous for that to happen to you.

Remember, you don't have to agree with them; you are merely stating it is reasonable and acceptable to feel the way they do. If people don't come flocking to you for your unique compliments, they might come for how you appear to understand and listen to them.

If people want advice, they'll ask. After all, it's not like the solutions to people's problems are incredibly creative and require ingenuity. People almost always know what they need to do to solve their problem; they just don't want to hear it from others prematurely.

They need to get to that point themselves, and a big part of the process is ranting and raving and thinking out loud.

So instead of giving unsolicited thoughts or advice, take a moment to ascertain the purpose of a person's statement. Make it a binary choice: does this person actually want my input, or are they just letting off steam and need an ear to scream into? There is a big difference between the two. If someone is asking for advice, let them ask specifically and explicitly. Otherwise, shut up and listen. If they don't ask you for specific advice or specific solutions, be content with being a simple sounding board.

There are two possible roles for you: a sounding board or an advice columnist. It's not hard to guess that the latter is far less welcome the majority of the time. Allow people to spill their guts to you and they'll begin to trust you with other things as well. Read into the context of what people are looking for and your repulsion factor will greatly decrease. Remember, it is so very rarely about you.

You Are Creepy

And before you say that this is just a male problem, it's not. This can apply equally to males and females. It just happens to manifest more in females because, well, you'll see.

You've heard people call others creepy before behind their backs. People may even say the same about you behind your back. Obviously, it's something you want to avoid that can cause far worse than awkward silence. But what does it really mean and how can you avoid it?

It turns out scientists have actually attempted to quantify "creepiness." The first theory comes to us from evolutionary psychologists, who tend to view much of our behavior through the lens that it helped us survive when we were still living in fear of wild animal attacks every day. More specifically, the feeling of dread or discomfort from creepy people is referred to as *agency detection*, which means you become aroused and alert if you sense danger. Of course, this is known as the *fight-*

or-flight instinct, which is the choices our body prepares itself for when danger is perceived.

So that's why the feeling of creepiness exists; what exactly is it looking for? If you are feeling negative from a gun pointed at you, that's not creepiness. If you are about to jump off of a bridge, that's not creepiness either. It can make your hairs stand up, give you goosebumps, and send chills down your spine. But it's still different. It isn't just emotional or physical harm that we want to steer clear of, even though those create feelings of danger and discomfort as well. No, creepiness is something that takes a very specific combination of factors to arouse.

A study from Knox College led by Francis McAndrew can lend some knowledge to this area. The researchers gave over 1300 participants a questionnaire on the traits and actions that would make them label someone "creepy." The questionnaire allowed the participants to rate sample behaviors, occupations, and even hobbies on a creepiness scale. The participants were both male and female (1029 females and 312 males), and they were able to generate five major actions that made someone get called the C word.

1. Appear to be watching and staring at someone before interacting with them.
2. Touching someone an inappropriate amount.
3. Frequently steering the conversation to sex.
4. Asking to take a picture of people alone.
5. Asking for personal details about someone's family.

Other actions that didn't make the top five include avoiding all eye contact and standing too close to someone and violating their personal space. Other findings include the fact that clowns, taxidermists, and funeral directors were seen as creepy occupations, and creepy hobbies included collecting dolls or insects and watching people (such as voyeurism).

Taking a step back, it's clear that all of these actions do indeed invoke the word creepiness. We make an uncomfortable face and cringe when we imagine someone doing it to us. The worst part is the perpetrators likely have no idea of the impression they are creating.

One of the common threads of all of the actions is that there is a sense of ambiguity and uncertainty. People weren't sure if they were truly in danger or should be alert—sometimes that's worse, isn't it? When you know you have a big speech in front of 1000 people, you can prepare yourself for it. But when there is an ambiguous threat, you don't know if it's coming or what form it might be in. Uncertainty about a threat evokes far worse fear. Unpredictability, while in other parts of this book can serve to invigorate you, compounds on dread and fear in the face of a potential threat. It also paralyzes us and leaves us unable to respond or act because we simply don't know what we should do.

There are countless other ways you can try to define or quantify creepiness, but deciphering the meaning of the word isn't the important part; understanding seven actions you should avoid is the important part.

You Always Laugh First

We all have fake laughs. No matter how honest we think we are or how much we hate sugarcoating things to people, we still utilize our fake laughs on a daily basis.

Here's the thing about most of us—we're inherently nice! We want people to like us, we want social situations to go smoothly, and we want awkward silences to die. Most importantly, we don't want people to feel bad about themselves when they inevitably make a bad joke. So we throw them a pity chuckle.

Fake laughter is the lubricant that salvages many conversations. It fills empty space and gives you something to do when you have no idea what to say. It keeps conversation rolling and gives the appearance of engagement even if you're bored out of your mind. Appearances, as it turns out, do matter sometimes. If you're speaking with the head honcho of your company, you know that your best fake laughter will be put to the test because you want them to like you.

And sometimes we depend on the fake

laughter of other people to prevent us from feeling self-conscious or stupid.

So we laugh at people's jokes. Laughter is pretty much an integral part of our daily lexicon—but that doesn't mean we like it, and the more we have to do it with someone, the more tiring—and ultimately unpleasant—it is to talk to them.

Obviously, fake laughter from others is something we want to avoid, so what is the biggest step we can take to prevent it? *Never laugh at your own jokes, at least not first.*

The biggest culprit for people to use their fake laughter and ultimately get tired of talking to you is when you laugh at your own joke loudly and proudly and without looking to the other person for a reaction—especially when the jokes aren't great—time after time. Think about it.

Monica makes a mediocre joke and laughs at it. Don't you feel like you have to give her a fake chuckle to keep the conversation moving and give her the reaction she is seeking?

Okay, so you force a smile onto your face and expel some breath from your lungs. No big deal. Then Monica does it again. And again. And again. And your facial muscles start to hurt because of how much you have to contort it into a fake, glazed-over smile. I'm annoyed just writing about it and I don't even know Monica. In person, I'm sure I would grow tired in record time and make an excuse to wander away from Monica.

That's what laughing at your own jokes first, without gauging how the other person receives it, will do to your conversation partners. When you always laugh first, you're *imposing your will* on the conversation partner and essentially telling them how to feel. You are showing them the emotion you want by demonstrating it, and it's hard to stray from that in normal conversation.

That's like talking about politics and then subtly telling them how you want them to vote. The worst part is that you aren't able to hear their opinions, so the conversation slowly becomes a platform for you to showcase your alleged humor—and that is not a conversation most people enjoy being a part of.

It's a very slippery slope to becoming "that guy" or "that girl" that people try to avoid at parties because they don't notice that a person wants to talk about something else besides their jokes.

There's also an element of the inability to read social cues if you're always laughing first, loudly, and proudly. Social cues are the little signs and hints people give off that say what they're really thinking. For example, a common social cue is that when someone leans back with their arms crossed and looks around the room behind you, they aren't interested in what you have to say. What cues can you observe if you're reacting first and forcing them to abandon their social cues to match you? You could be throwing your head back in laughter while the other person is slowly inching away and you might not even notice.

Another element to always laughing first at your own jokes is it leaves you completely unable to gauge how funny you actually are.

Without any proper and uninfluenced reactions, you are living in a world where you only hear laughter—laughter of your own that you manufacture. This can lead to an inflated sense of self—I'm sure you have friends that think they are hilarious because all they do is hear their own laughter.

Others might laugh with you, but it doesn't mean they think you're funny. Always laughing first is usually a reaction born out of insecurity and the fear of conversational rejection, which is essentially silence after a joke. You start by wanting to *seed* laughter and make sure that you get the response you are looking for, and after a while, it becomes a subconscious habit you can't break out of.

Not getting the emotional reaction that you want can be embarrassing or downright paralyzing to some people, so it makes sense that they want to seed the emotion, in a sense. It's understandable and we've all felt it when we were feeling shy or nervous about something—nervous laughter, anyone?

But remember the burden and feeling you are creating in others when you laugh first, at yourself, without gauging the response in others. After all, it's hard to listen and observe when your mouth is making noise. The realization that you may be hamstringing conversation with this simple no-no can be transformational.

Takeaways:

- You could be the most interesting person in the world and no one will care if you have annoying or repulsive conversational habits. Indeed, sometimes it is better to be more benign and less offensive.
- Annoying habit number one is to see things as only black and white, judge people, and try to control what they think. People will begin to avoid you.
- Annoying habit number two is to provide your unsolicited thoughts and advice to people when they only want you to listen and validate them. Understand what people are seeking from you before answering or people will begin to avoid you.
- Annoying habit number three is creepy behaviors, which occur in both genders.

Creepy behaviors have to do with making people uncomfortable with the amount of attention and focus they receive.
- Annoying habit number four is always laughing first instead of gauging people's reactions and letting them decide their humor for themselves. This is usually done out of insecurity and serves to impose your will on others.

Chapter 8. Self-Defense

This is the chapter of self-defense, which might be the first thing that popped into your head as you read the title, *Conversation Tactics*. Truth be told, conversation tactics are handy and helpful when you are trying to make a positive impression, but they are doubly important when you need to defend your space or stance.

Put another way, it's more important to have a shield to protect yourself than a sword to make an attack, because protecting yourself (conversationally, figuratively, literally, psychologically) takes higher priority. In any case, this is a chapter where we introduce some tactics and maneuvers to work your way around foes and *frenemies* alike. These are the techniques that allow you to say what you want without ruffling feathers and glide in and out of situations with grace—or at least just make sure you aren't being taken advantage of and laughed at behind your back.

How to Say No

Let's suppose you own a pickup truck. One day, you hear that your friend Jack is moving apartments and looking for people to help him.

You must know that you've got a bulls-eye target on your back because of your truck. Jack has moved four times in the past year and he's come to you every single time. He didn't pay, and he only bought you a Hawaiian pizza with pineapple that had a questionable odor.

You don't mind helping people and you have a good heart. But why do you keep moving Jack's couch and piano with him when you know it's a terrible idea with no redeeming qualities? You know why—you have a fear of telling people no.

Learning to say no can be the ultimate defensive skill a person can possess. Most of us aim to please. We've often found that it can be easier to say yes than to say no. When we say no, we realize that we bring negativity and possible confrontation or disappointment into an interaction.

There are some main reasons that people don't like to say no:

- We're afraid of being rude.
- We want to be agreeable. We don't want to alienate ourselves from the individual or the group making the request.
- We're afraid of conflict. Maybe the person or persons making the request will get angry if we reject their request. This might lead to an ugly or unpleasant confrontation. Many of us try to avoid confrontations as much as possible.
- We don't want to burn bridges. Some people take no as a sign of personal rejection and they may decide to hold your lack of cooperation against you.
- We like to be helpful. It feels good. But at what price? Our time is valuable.

But consider that the people forcing you to say no don't care about any of that—in fact, they're banking on the fact that you care more than they do. What do you believe will happen when you say no? Will you be burned at the stake? Chances are low. Hanged in effigy? Executed? Probably not.

One simple way to say no more easily and often is to change the vocabulary you use. *The Journal of Consumer Research* published a study in which 120 students were divided into two groups—the "I can't" group and the "I don't" group. One group was told that each time they were faced with temptation they were to tell themselves, "I can't do X." For example, when tempted with chocolate, they were to say, "I can't eat chocolate." The other group, the "I don't" group, was instructed to say, "I don't do X" or, in the case of chocolate, "I don't eat chocolate."

The results of this study showed the major impact that just a slight difference in vocabulary can make on our ability to say no, to resist temptation, and to motivate goal-directed behavior. The "I don't" group was overwhelming more successful in its ability to say no.

"I can't" becomes an exercise in self-discipline. but when you tell yourself "I don't," you're creating a line in the sand that takes the situation out of your hands. Your choice was premade to say no and thus you can stick to it more easily. By simply changing one word when we talk to ourselves, we can change our behavior. When people hear "don't," it's more of a hard boundary, whereas "can't" typically implies an open-ended answer that encourages people to try to persuade and coax you.

In learning to say no, the same "I don't" principle applies to someone who gets repeated requests for favors or obligations. Instead of reviewing each request separately, you might consider rejecting the entire category. In other words, instead of reviewing each request and making an "I can" or an "I can't" decision, you'll find that it's much more empowering to reject all requests that are in a certain category, such as "Sorry, I don't do those types of meetings anymore."

Refusing an entire category is a boundary that most people will accept. If they sense you make exceptions frequently, they will attempt to persuade you to let them be yet another one.

The toughest time in saying no usually occurs right after you do so. It's then when you want to offer help, keep talking, or do anything to reduce the tension that your no has created. This is usually the time when you start wavering: "Well, if you really need my help, I guess I could . . ." "I'd rather not, but . . ." Resist the temptation and stay silent, because your assertiveness is often lost in that moment. This is the moment where your façade of assertiveness can easily break—but remember, all you need to do is get past this split second of immense tension and you will be home free.

If you still feel the need to add a "because" at the end of your sentence, keep it short and simple and don't elaborate on the details. The more details you give, the more fodder you give people to pick at. For instance, if you say no to helping a friend move because you need to walk your cat in the morning, you create an avenue for people to dispute that you need to walk a cat at all.

Don't hem and haw your way through an explanation on why you said no. Don't feel compelled to share an alternative or something that can make up for your no. It's okay to just say no. No further explanation is needed. Overall, remember that no can be a complete sentence.

If you can't just say no or if you can't say no immediately, another option is to defer the decision or punt it into the future. Tell them you'll think about it, and then ask them to follow up. In other words, put the burden back on them by requesting something to help you consider their request.

Let's take Jonathan, who is very smart and mentors companies. He is asked for coffee all the time from people who would like to "pick his brain" and otherwise soak up information from him like a sponge. He has to say no quite frequently, but he's devised a way around it. He creates a hoop for them to jump through before agreeing to anything further.

When someone asks him for coffee, he will ask them to send, via email, an agenda or plan of what they want to discuss and why. He doesn't hear from 99% of the people again.

When someone asks you for something, create a condition for them to fulfill in order for you to consider their request. It will buy you time and space, and most people will never get back to you because they would have to put in the work.

Another option, if you're having a tough time saying no, will be to offer a bait and switch yes: "I can't do that, but I can do this."

"I can't spend all day helping you move to another apartment, but I can give you one hour."

"I can't go out with you this weekend, but I promise that I'll make some time to do that within the next month."

"I can't serve on the board, but I'll be willing to consult on an ad-hoc basis whenever I have time."

What you're doing here is saying no to the request and offering a smaller consolation prize that may or may not be refused. It may be a legitimate alternative as something you are willing to do, but it doesn't have to be. Your no is disguised because you appear to be still open and willing, at least on the surface. If you offer something relatively small, people will likely refuse and tell you not to bother with it.

Even better is if you don't provide specific detail and leave it as open-ended as possible. In most cases, the bait and switch will result in freedom from an ask or obligation. This tactic alleviates most of the tension because you are saying yes to something, just not what is specifically being asked.

A final way to tell people no is to *pass the buck*. Here, you aren't saying no as much as "Yes, but . . ." Allow me to explain. Passing the buck means passing the responsibility onto someone else who is not you.

It's when you suggest that someone else would be a much better, more qualified fit than you, and thus, you should bow out. You wouldn't do the requester justice, but you can still help them solve their problem by finding someone who will. The requester won't necessarily hear a no, which is the most important part.

For instance, if you are asking someone to drive you to the airport, you might say, "No, I'm a terrible driver and driving on the highways make me feel anxious, but Ted is a great driver and might be free that day!" You've successfully passed the buck to Ted by making yourself pale in comparison to how Ted might solve the issue.

People ask you for things because they want to solve a problem they have. If you make yourself seem like a terrible solution, but at the same time can point them in the direction of a real solution, you've avoided a duty.

Saying no is a valuable skill. In learning to say no, you'll be able to take control of your life and your time. In learning to say no, you'll empower yourself to avoid the things you don't want to do. In learning to say no properly, you'll be able to avoid tension, confrontation, and ruffled feathers. A life devoid of no is one that is not your own; it is one that is lived for other people.

If you've been passive for a long time, people are going to be surprised when you say no. And if you're dealing with someone who has an alpha personality, they will almost surely try to get you to change your decision. Heck, your lack of assertiveness might by why they hang around you in the first place, and it's tough to change that relationship dynamic once it's been set. Expect pushback and shock when you change the dynamic.

How to Deflect and Roll with the Punches

As a former fat kid, I used to have a fairly extensive library of witty comebacks for those charming people who liked to point out that I was, indeed, still as fat as I was the day before. Or that they couldn't ride in a car with me for fear of it tipping over. Or that I was so big my Polo brand sport shirt had a *real* horse on it. (This one was pretty clever, I'll admit. Kids really become innovators when they want to insult someone.)

Mind you, I wasn't really that large—just 20 pounds overweight. Luckily for me, it didn't carry over too much into adulthood. It's probably best characterized as extreme "baby fat" fueled by too much candy.

Unlike many of my peers in fatness, the teasing didn't bother me too much. That's because the bullies mostly stopped picking on me because I developed an arsenal of comebacks whenever I was insulted. These comebacks never failed to either shut people up or bring them to my side through laughter. It's no wonder that a common origin story for comedians is awkward childhoods where they were bullied, forcing them to defend themselves with their sense of humor. For instance:

You're so fat that horse on your shirt is life-sized!
Comeback: You're wrong. It's WAY bigger. Were you also aware that my Polo sport shirt can be used as a parachute?

Better not ride with Patrick. He's going to tip the car over!

Comeback: You better put six extra wheels on your car for me!

Becoming a witty comeback machine is easier than you think, and it's one of the best conversation tactics you can learn. It doesn't only rear its head when dealing with insults—it is widely applicable once you learn the framework. If it's a bad situation, a witty comeback can diffuse the tension and bring emotional levels back to normal. If it's a good situation, then a witty comeback can make it even jollier.

Whatever the situation, mastering witty comebacks will earn you the respect of other people for your clever wit. It just takes one line—and the shorter and punchier, the better and more effective. A witty comeback does many things simultaneously. It makes people laugh and disarms them while allowing you to appear smart, insightful, and mentally quick.

What did the examples above do? They didn't fight the insult. Rather, they went along with it and even amplified it. They played along and poked fun at themselves as if they were the bully's minion. By taking the insult head-on and rolling with it, they disarmed the bully, who actually wanted a negative reaction instead of assistance. All expectations were defied, and it was even a little bit funny.

That sneaky and subtle way of defending yourself is the definition of a witty comeback. You take a statement and use it as an opportunity to show wit and grace in disarming someone, as opposed to head-to-head conflict. The above examples could easily have been replied to with "I'm not even that fat. Leave me alone!" or "Well, what about your haircut?" You can imagine how these wouldn't disarm anyone and indeed would create tension and encourage bullying. In fact, you might make someone want to sock you in the face.

Witty comebacks aren't just for disarming people and easing tension, however. The nature of interaction with friends is that we make fun of each other harder than any bully ever will. Exercising these muscles will make your comebacks better and quicker, instead of having to text them to people 20 minutes after the insult was slung.

We'll get to how to construct a couple of bulletproof witty comebacks, but first, a few words of caution when dealing with this type of fire.

First, generic is bad. You know generic when you hear it, and don't be that person who uses jokes that their grandparent might use. For instance, "I know you are, but what am I?" or "So is your mom."

A witty comeback is judged by how funny or original it is. Using something that is generic or unclever is decidedly neither funny nor creative. Don't just use a generic or template-driven witty comeback that you've seen in a movie or something that better works in a totally unrelated context. And don't use one of the comebacks you thought were hilarious when you were 10. They don't work anymore.

Second, don't act like you can't take a joke.

Of course, witty comebacks need an initial statement to "come back" to. The vast majority of the time, people are indeed joking when they say something negative about you in your presence. For some people, it's their main way of interacting with friends. It's almost a compliment because they assume you have a sufficient sense of humor and the emotional resiliency to deal with it. Go figure.

Any way you slice it, it's a mode of communication you should have in your bag. The people who *aren't* involved in jokes and good-natured ribbing don't have many friends. If you let it show that you are angry or hurt, it spoils the playful tone you could otherwise enhance with your witty comeback. People think they can joke with you, and you might just prove them 100% incorrect.

For example, if someone made a joke about my fatness, and I got visibly angry, they would likely stop but walk on eggshells around me for days. When someone is uncomfortable with something, they make others uncomfortable as well. If that happens enough times, they'll eventually stop engaging me. Handle the initial negative statement with a wry smirk and with the knowledge that you are about to crush them. Roll with it and dish something back their way.

Third, use the right tone. The best witty comebacks are delivered with 50% indifference. You should never be too excited to thwart someone because that too will show that you are affected by their initial insult.

Indifference is the correct tone because comebacks are about showing that you are cool as a cucumber and whipping out your hidden weapon. If it helps, pretend that you are James Bond delivering a witty retort after a failed murder attempt by a villain. A witty comeback is the verbal equivalent of judo or aikido—using an opponent's words against them. If you take that analogy, you need a certain amount of cool to effectively counteract. Witty comebacks take the power away from the insult hurled.

There are three main types of witty comeback. None are better than the other, but some might come easier to you more naturally and comfortably.

Type #1: Agree and amplify. The idea here is to agree with whatever the insult was and then add to it in an absurd way. You amplify the initial sentiment to a degree that is ridiculous. This was my go-to technique to deflect jokes about my weight. If their sentiment is X, then your sentiment should try to be 10X. You are joining in the party against yourself but also showing security because you are making yourself a bigger butt of the joke.

If you forgot from earlier in this chapter: *You're so fat that horse on your shirt is life-sized!*

Amplification: *Were you also aware that my Polo sport shirt can be used as a parachute?*

Bob: *Your cooking was pretty terrible last time.*
Amplification: *You're lucky you didn't stay until the end of the night. We all got our stomachs pumped. Dinner at my place later tonight?*

Type #2: Reverse and amplify. This is a simple deflection. This is when you get back at them in a subtle way. When someone says you are bad at X, you basically turn it around by saying that they are even worse at X. It's the exact same as the previous type of witty comeback, except instead of directing the amplification at yourself, you direct it to the other person.

Bob: *Your cooking was pretty terrible last time.*
You: *Yeah, but at least I didn't need to get my stomach pumped the way I did after you cooked last time!*

Johnny: *Those shoes are so ugly.*
You: *Yeah, but at least the color of mine don't cause blindness like yours!*

Type #3: Use an outlandish comparison. This brings the conversation into a different sphere and makes both people laugh at the weird outlandish imagery. Go oddball, extreme, and over the top. To use the same framework, you're amplifying (to yourself or the other person) with an analogy here. This doesn't quite throw it back at them; it just deflects and changes the topic out of absurdity and even confusion.

Bob: *Your cooking was pretty terrible last time.*
You: *True, I should have used the eggs as hockey pucks, right?*

Johnny: *Those shoes are so ugly.*
You: *They make you look like Cindy Crawford's beauty mark.*

Witty comebacks are the blood of witty banter, which is being able to take an element of what was said and attack it from a different angle without missing a beat. You should be able to see how this can play out. They are instant retorts that aren't hostile or combative while addressing something gracefully. What more can you ask for?

Word of caution: fight the temptation to rattle them off one after the other. Again, you have to remember that your goal is to get people to like you. You're not trying to prove a point or protect your pride. Too much makes it feel like you are one-dimensional and can't hold a substantive conversation.

Firing off one comeback after another can kill whatever level of comfort you've managed to create because you will appear insecure, defensive, and full of bluster.

Roll with the punches a bit more and you'll see one of two things: joy in people's eyes as they realize they can engage you in that way or terror in people's eyes as they realize they won't be able to keep up with you.

According to a study on the role of humor in sexual selection conducted by anthropologist Gil Greengross, self-importance and pomposity were found to be the traits most despised in potential sexual mates. In fact, he found that "Self-deprecating humour [sic] can be an especially reliable indicator not only of general intelligence and verbal creativity, but also of moral virtues such as humility." Keep that in mind.

Always Admit Wrong

When we defend ourselves, we usually go in with the mindset that we have to win. After all, otherwise, we lose whatever we are defending. And for us to do so, we plan to lay down only accurate facts, put forward the correct line of reasoning, and say all the right things. Our defense has to be iron-clad from errors and mistakes, and we must never have to say, *"I don't know"* or *"I'm wrong."*

But contrary to this common assumption of ours is a suggestion for an altogether counterintuitive approach for winning arguments: *plan to admit you're wrong at least once during the argument.*

Now why on Earth would you want to give your opponent ammunition by way of clearly showcasing an error in your thinking or a flaw in your argument? Simple: it builds people's confidence in the rest of the things you do state to be right. It makes your words count and builds your credibility. Plus, by admitting you're wrong, you're showing that you're not a childish, egotistic gabber but a sensible, mature conversationalist.

Think of people you know who have occasionally admitted they were wrong or didn't know all the details about something. When they did state things they knew to be true, don't you trust their words all the more? It's precisely because you know they're the kind of people who honestly admit their mistakes that you now have more confidence in the things they declare as true. Moreover, you'll tend to have a higher respect for them after seeing how sensibly they handled what could've easily been an awkward situation. When you do this to others, you disarm them and make their offense less vicious and malicious. When people realize they are speaking with a human and not an immovable brick wall, they will revert to acting human themselves. This benefits your defensive efforts.

Say you're in the meeting room, trying to convince the group that the best venue for the company's product launch is outdoors, and not indoors as some of your colleagues have suggested. Plan to bring up a point you know the other side will refute for being wrong (e.g., "*The clubhouse is big enough 100 people, so that should be enough to accommodate our guests*"). Once they correct you ("*Actually we're expecting at least 150 guests*"), say, "*Sorry, I was wrong. If that's the case, maybe we can use the garden venue instead. It has a more open feel, better-suited for a larger guest list."*

So as you see, while it may pain you to have to say "*I'm wrong*" for fear that it will ruin your credibility, this move is actually something that'll help increase people's trust in you and maybe even better drive your point home. Saying "*I'm wrong*" or "*I don't know*" shows people you have the insight enough to recognize when you have to surrender the battle and the wisdom enough to know that some battles need to be lost in order to win the war.

Dealing with Passive-Aggressiveness

You and a colleague at the office have opposing views on how to go about a project. While you suggest starting off with a fundraiser to finance the project, he wants to dive right into the project headfirst, taking the funds from the company savings. After much deliberation with the rest of your team, your idea wins and you're assigned as the project leader. Your colleague says sure, he'll help carry out the plans you've proposed. He's assigned key tasks to do for the fundraiser and he seems enthusiastic about following through.

But he never does. He misses connecting with the people he should've contacted weeks ago. Meetings with sponsors he was supposed to hold never push through. The flyers for the fundraiser remain undone. None of these misfires happens through his fault, of course. There's always some other person, a technical problem, a miscommunication, or a storm somewhere that's to blame for the tasks remaining undone. Honest to God—he's doing his best. He's sorry your plans don't seem to be working out. Tough luck.

Tough luck, indeed—not because you're working with someone who may have broken a mirror and is now suffering terrible luck but because you're likely working with someone who's passive-aggressive.

Referred to by clinical psychologist Albert Bernstein as "emotional vampires," passive-aggressives are people who suck you dry and then act like they're the victims. Unable to directly assert their opinions or express their honest feelings, they instead resort to underhanded tactics to get what they want or get their message across. They won't tell you they disagree with your ideas or plans. They'll opt to sabotage you instead by "forgetting" to do things or "misunderstanding" your instructions. They won't tell you they feel disappointed or angry. Instead, they'll cancel an important meeting because they're "sick" or "accidentally" feed a vital document to the paper shredder.

In their minds, none of the things they've done or failed to do were intentional. They believe they're innocent people doing what they can, and it's life or fate or maybe even you that's causing them to fail. If you call them out for their shortcomings or hint that their behaviors seem to constitute sabotage, they're hurt and accuse you of bullying or being an inconsiderate, selfish prick.

So how do you deal with passive-aggressives in a way that won't have you end up getting a written reprimand from HR or spending time in jail? Erik Barker, citing insight from Bernstein, lists five ways.

First, don't hand over what they want on a silver platter. It may seem easier to simply give in to what they want to happen (read: you take all the blame and do all the work, while they're let off the hook) than continue having to clean up after their mess, but you're not doing yourself any favor by allowing it. You're only encouraging them to continue such behavior, because you let them get away with it the last time.

Second, don't ever call them out or get angry at them. Remember, in their minds, none of the bad things that have happened is their fault. They have a distorted view of the world and their way of dealing with it, so if you call them out and remind them of their accountability, they won't see your logic no matter how nicely you put it. If you get angry at them, no matter how justified you think that anger is, they will only see it as an attack.

Third, understand and speak their language. When talking with them, remember their frame of reference: themselves as well-meaning, innocent victims. They feel they've been treated unfairly by the world, and the logical reaction they're supposed to get from others for having to suffer that is kindness and consideration. They think of themselves as deserving of sympathy and understanding, so make sure you communicate that. Tell your colleague you understand how difficult it is to set up that meeting when those sponsors just aren't available all the time. Acknowledge his efforts, then provide him concrete steps on how to go about the task. Praise even failed efforts; point out that those are signs he's trying and you appreciate him doing so.

Fourth, be clear about what you want them to do and reward them for doing it. Relying only on unspoken expectations is a surefire way to grant passive-aggressives the key to driving you crazy. If you want them to deliver on something, be clear about how you want it done and by when. When they do follow through on the tasks, heap on approval and praise. Make them feel that they have a lot more to gain (especially status and widespread acclaim) from helping you than sabotaging you. Despite seeming like they're always upset with the world, passive-aggressives actually crave acceptance and approval most of all. If you make them feel that you think highly of them and value their contributions, they might just start seeing you as an ally rather than a foe.

Finally, if nothing else works, your last resort is to increase the cost of failing to deliver. This doesn't mean you break out the lashing whip and impose unreasonable punishments for offenses. This just means making messing up more inconvenient for passive-aggressives, like having them do over substandard work, requiring incident reports, or increasing the value of things they're trying to avoid. For example, if your colleague serially misses only those meetings related to your fundraiser (but mysteriously gets to attend the rest), inform him that decisions directly affecting him are being made during your meetings. His absence means he's failing to take a vote, thus having him take on more unpleasant tasks than he needs to.

Dealing with passive-aggressive people is a skill that you may wish you don't have to learn, but you're likely gonna have to. One of the most difficult parts of it may be swallowing your pride to express sympathy and understanding instead of exasperation or anger toward them, but it's the only way to move forward when you're dealing with this type of people. Otherwise, you'll only be fanning the flames or, worse, matching their game and becoming passive-aggressive yourself. To prevent this from happening, you'll need to be aware of how you're responding to them and continually check that you're doing so appropriately.

Takeaways:

- Dealing with people is not always easy because some of those people don't have the best of intentions toward you. In that case, it's important to understand how to defend yourself in conversation and keep your cool.
- One of the first ways to defend yourself is to defend your space and time. That's through learning how to gracefully say no to people, places, and things. You can do this through your phrasing, creating categories, passing the buck, and creating hoops for people to jump through. These are all ways of avoiding a direct no that

might offend someone.
- Deflecting insults and ridicule is also important to master. These are otherwise known as witty comebacks and make you part of the joke instead of the butt. The easiest ways to deflect insults are to use amplification or to redirect to something outlandish, both of which take the attention off you.
- Plan to admit you are wrong at least once during each argument or each occasion you are defending yourself. Your defense is more credible if you admit wrongdoing or fault, and it makes people lower their guards once they realize they're not going up against a brick wall.
- Passive-aggressive people are the worst. So here's a method for dealing with them. Don't give them what they want, don't get angry at them, speak their language of feeling wronged, give them clear incentives to act, and increase the cost for failure to comply.

Chapter 9. On the Offensive

In contrast to the following chapter of being defensive, this is a chapter that is more akin to the proverbial or conversational sword. It's about how to argue effectively, prove your point, and get your way more often than not.

After you feel secure in defending your psyche or thoughts, the next step isn't to contentedly stay still in regards to others. There are always situations in life that we shy away from because we aren't comfortable with confrontation. If you gave a poll to 100 people, I would wager that confrontation, public speaking, and heights are the fears that would be the most common.

We just don't like going on the offense because we are never sure if we are justified on what we are doing or saying. What if we're wrong, and what if they think we're stupid?

Those are always possibilities, but one of the realizations about confrontation is that when we avoid it, we eventually paint ourselves into a mental prison that is of our own doing. We eventually let just about everything slide in the interest of avoiding conflict, and that's a very lonely existence. How can we embody some of the better practices of argumentation and confrontation, and how to make it so if you don't get your way, at least you aren't being trampled over.

Best Practices

You come home, tired from work, and see that your husband still hasn't arranged for the plumber to fix your sink, even though you've already reminded him about it several times. You feel that he's not carrying his share of the load in your relationship, which you take as a sign that he's losing interest in you. If he really cared about you and your relationship, he'd remember to take care of the things you've asked him to do, right?

The thought pushes you to the edge of annoyance, flirting with the line toward anger. You spot him in the bedroom, glued to his phone. You confront him about the sink. "*Sorry, honey, I forgot. I'll take care of it tomorrow,*" he says without looking up from his phone. You feel even more ignored and sense the blood rising up the back of your neck. This is about to turn into a fight, and you gear up to throw the first punch (figuratively—maybe).

Arguments can happen in every relationship. Connect the lives of two individuals who have differing backgrounds, needs, values, perspectives, and ways of communicating, and here you have the ingredients for conflict. But those ingredients don't necessarily have to be cooked into a cold dish of disappointment, misery, and regret. You can learn a recipe for turning a point of conflict into a potential for growth, a ruinous argument into an effective conversation.

To deal with conflict constructively, Eric Ravenscraft suggests that you first have to recognize that each conflict consists of two problem aspects: *the situation and the emotion*. In the above scenario, the problem situation is that the sink needs fixing, and the problem emotion is your feeling of frustration toward your partner for not getting it done. Your frustration then got compounded by your sense of being ignored, which hurt you, turning your emotion into anger.

Now consider what's likely to happen if you try to resolve the problem situation without first addressing the problem emotion. Chances are, what'll ensue will be an argument fueled by the problem emotion (i.e., anger) instead of a mature conversation focused on resolving the problem situation. This is how couples end up having fights that drag in all other past offenses completely unrelated to the present situation—what's taken control is the problem emotion, while the problem situation has been completely swept to the side.

To avoid having this kind of argument that ultimately accomplishes nothing but increasing the resentment of each partner toward the other, Dr. Lerner suggests dealing with the two problem aspects separately.

First, deal with the problem emotion. If you feel angry, take a moment to calm yourself down. Take slow, deep breaths, go for a walk, or write your anger out on a piece of paper, then burn it. Don't just take off with your partner clueless about what you're trying to do, though. Before you institute your self-prescribed anger management ritual, it's best if you've informed your significant other that you just need to take a breather so that you can deal with the situation better later.

Once you've calmed down enough, make sure you return to your partner, this time to resolve the second part of the problem: the situation. Because you've managed the problem emotion, you're now better able to approach the situation rationally and with an open mind. When you do discuss with your significant other, take the stance of a collaborative partner. Act to find a win-win solution for both parties instead of insisting that you must win the fight and rub defeat in your opponent's face. When you take the collaborative approach, you avoid having a messy argument and instead hold a discussion that helps both parties feel heard and arrive at a solution.

So just how do you carry out a conversation with your partner that's collaborative, solution-oriented, and makes them feel truly heard? Psychologist and relationship expert Dr. Shannon Kolakowski recommends the following three-step approach: ask, validate, and join.

First, ask. This step is about asking your partner whether you've understood their point correctly. This will need you to paraphrase what your partner has just said, then ask them if you got it right. For example, say, *"What I'm hearing is that you feel controlled when I constantly nag you about household chores. Is this what you're trying to say?"* Most arguments escalate to irredeemable heights because each person piles on a counterargument without first truly understanding what the other person just said. Asking for clarifications and seeking to listen first before itching to launch a counterattack helps the conversation move forward in a productive way.

Second, validate. Once you have a good grasp of how your partner views the problem, validate their emotions about it. This doesn't mean you should agree with everything they're saying just to give an end to the argument. Validating means acknowledging the person's right to feel the way they feel and communicating an understanding of why they may feel or see the situation that way. To do this, you might say, *"Given the situation, it's completely understandable that you'd feel that way."* This helps your partner feel that they're not talking to a wall after all, that their concerns are being heard and considered in a legitimate way.

Third, join. This step is what truly transforms you and your partner from two people discussing their thoughts and feelings with one another to a collaborative partnership determined to resolve the conflict and improve the relationship. Joining eliminates the "you against me" stance and replaces it with the "we against the problem" outlook.

This creates a team mindset, reminding you that the enemy is not each other, but the problem at hand. In this step, you might say, *"I want the same things you do—to make this relationship work and move forward with a better understanding each other. We can both figure out how to do this together."* This brings your relationship to the forefront, reminding both of you to focus on it as your main concern and not on the background noise of anger, pride, and selfishness that ring loud in every argument if you so allow.

As you go through the steps of asking, validating, and joining with your partner, remember to leave your ego outside the door. The entire process is not so that you could have the last word or win the argument for yourself, but so that you could find a common ground where you and your significant other can build a stronger relationship.

Moreover, in the course of your conversation, stick to stating the facts instead of throwing evaluations at your partner. For instance, saying *"I've asked you to contact the plumber twice, and both times you said you were going to call him*" is stating a fact. On the other hand, saying "*You never take care of things around the house*" is an evaluation. You may see how bringing up such an evaluation may be taken by your partner as an unfair accusation; maybe he does help out around the house, just not in the way you expected. So to avoid inciting negative reactions, steer clear of evaluations.

As an alternative to stating evaluations, use "I feel" statements. For example, instead of declaring "*You never take care of things around the house*," say, "*I feel frustrated when things I expected to be taken care of are not done.*" This way of stating the problem shows your partner that you recognize how your own expectations are playing a role in the frustration that you feel instead of putting all the blame for it on him.

After stating how you feel about the situation, the next question in the other person's mind is typically "*Well, what could I have done better?*" Some arguments never end because one person fixates on the wrong that's been done and keeps drilling into the other what shouldn't be done in the future.

Thus, the conversation never moves forward to what *can* be done to remedy the situation.

Avoid falling into that fixation trap by framing your statements using positive language. State what you want to happen, such as *"It would mean a lot to me if you do things when you say you will, or at least tell me when you'll be unable to do it so we can work out a different arrangement."* This way, the other person knows how to proceed moving forward instead of being stuck in a labyrinth of blame.

Finally, when your partner's temper still flares despite your best efforts to keep the conversation calm and constructive, remember to have empathy. Imagine what it would be like being the person your partner is, and consider their reactions from their own view, given their respective histories and personalities. Is he taking the facts you're stating as offensive comments on his behavior? Maybe he's reacting that way because of deeper insecurities influenced by his past negative experiences and triggered by the situation.

Keep in mind that while conflicts and arguments can happen in every relationship, they don't need to be catastrophic events that bring your partnership to ruin. Ultimately, it's up to how you handle those first few biting remarks or moments of icy silence that'll spell the difference between a tumultuous breakup and a well-nurtured companionship.

No Ad Hominem

Arguments are inevitable, even with your best friends and significant other. Actually, they might occur even more with them.

But time after time, studies, most famously by John Gottman, have shown that how effectively and efficiently you resolve conflict with someone is a sign of how long those relationships will last. Graceful and effective conflict resolution is the topic for another book, but there is one golden rule that you must abide by: no ad hominem attacks.

Ad hominem is the Latin term for an attack on the person. In fact, that's the literal meaning of ad hominem: *to the man* or *against the man.* In other words, an ad hominem attack is making a personal attack on the other person that is unrelated to the point at hand.

It was originally coined for a debate tactic where a person arguing with another person attacks that person's character instead of that person's argument or logic. The hope is the person being attacked would spend too much time protecting his or her character that they drop their argument altogether.

In a sense, it's a smokescreen for the attacker to escape the original issue and live another day. If you hear someone attacking you on this basis, just know that they are grasping at straws and have nothing else to say. It's a sign of weakness. Here's a typical ad hominem argument:

Lisa, you forgot to get gas for the car again. Could you next time, please?

What about you? At least I can afford it, unlike you. How's your so-called job?

Note that the challenge is not against the

validity or soundness of the argument. Indeed, it doesn't even acknowledge or address it. The attack is against the person making the proposal, and the emotional reaction might indeed make the first speaker forget about the gas issue. Not every ad hominem is as obvious and blatant as this example. Most, in fact, are subtle and difficult to detect.

Ad hominems are logical fallacies; they are dirty tricks. They have no place at all in conversations. They can be incredibly toxic and are often the hallmark of someone that can't take responsibility for their own actions. They might not even realize what they're doing is massively deflecting any fault of their own.

There are jokes that come off like ad hominems. And I've already covered in the earlier parts of this book how you should handle those jokes. Simply agree with the joke, exaggerate it, and it will go away.

An ad hominem, on the other hand, is an insult. It's just meant to put you down. It's all about attacking a person's character. Here are ad hominem mistakes to avoid or be aware of—or, alternatively, to use frequently.

Going over their head. This is where you give the impression that you are above the other person in terms of intelligence, social class, or ability.

I would reply to that, but I'm not sure you'll get it. What you're saying is that the person is too stupid or too intellectually deficient to understand the reply you'd like to make.

Even you can get it. The *even you* assumes that you are at a high point, but more importantly that the other person is at an extremely low point. You are telling that person that there are ideas that even idiots can get, and since they are an idiot, they should get it.

I used to think that way. You are telling that person that you used to think like them, but not anymore. Now you're no longer stupid and mentally challenged like them.

Wishful thinking. This is when you impose an alternative explanation that's demeaning to the thought processes of the person you're talking to. You then try to rationalize why they think the way they think.

You think that way because you were abused as a child, weren't you? This is dismissive and insulting. You are saying the person is wrong but should be excused because that person is psychologically damaged. It's a double whammy.

Agreeing 100% is impossible, but there's certainly a healthy way to discuss these differences. Keeping ad hominem attacks to the minimum is a large aspect of the healthy method.

Appeal to Perfection

As all conversations have the seeds for a potential debate, it's important to know how to argue and defend yourself. If you are caught flat-footed and unready when you need to defend yourself, it will be very easy for people to steamroll you. If this happens repeatedly, especially in public, prepare for people's respect for you to plummet and the judgments to rise.

More often than not, arguments depend on tricks and logical fallacies that don't hold up when put to higher scrutiny. Remember, logical fallacies never address the core of the issue being argued. People who resort to them are not really engaging in argumentation. Instead, they are trying to cover their lack of knowledge or reason with deceptive tricks that make it appear like they are winning.

One of the most common argumentation tricks people will try to pull on you is an appeal to perfection. They will refute your argument because, according to them, what you propose is not the *perfect* solution. And anything that isn't perfect is not worth doing.

This way of arguing ignores the fact that there are intermediary solutions—solutions that are less than perfect but are nonetheless practical. By appealing to a perfect "be-all, end-all" solution, they make it seem that your argument is defective. In reality, you're just being practical. The appeal to perfection also takes any argument to an illogical conclusion, which is never reasonable to plan for.

An example is simply *Why should I shower? I'm just going to need another shower in a day or two.*

This is an appeal to perfection, with the implication being a shower should clean you once and for all time. It ignores the intermediary benefits of a shower. There are obvious alternatives to being 100% clean and 100% dirty. Never showering is an unreasonable conclusion drawn that is supposed to prove a point.

If you pursue this kind of reasoning to its logical conclusion, you'll get absurd and ridiculous results. One might as well argue that you should not eat today because you will be hungry again tomorrow anyway. But the reason it works is because people don't notice that the argument has been framed in a black and white manner.

This tactic tends to irritate people because the person using it jumps to conclusions that involve perfect states. The person making this argument ignores everything that is short of that perfect state. Nothing is ever good enough for that person, so you might as well drop your argument. It really creates a refutation for everything.

This is frustrating because it's dismissive while at the same time not really addressing anything. The other person hasn't offered a solution; they have just torn yours down in a way that isn't productive.

The appeal to perfection tactic is usually used by those that can't seem to offer alternative solutions. Their focus is on being correct, and technically they can almost always be correct by an appeal to perfection. They're correct like a stopped clock is correct twice a day.

Sowing Seeds of Doubt

This is a sneaky way of arguing because it can seem innocent and subtle. Even the name, sowing seeds of doubts, conjures an image of a secret agent lying in wait for years for his plans to come to fruition. The secret agent might integrate and appear to be a member of your society, so this argument method can be difficult to see sometimes.

Basically, the person looks at your argument and nitpicks at the smallest weaknesses and uncertainties while ignoring the greater benefits, no matter how irrelevant the flaw might be. It can be phrased as an innocent question, which disarms you. This person is essentially trying to undermine your confidence in the solution that you bring to the table.

At first glance, this appears more legitimate than other methods of arguing. They might actually have a point regarding those details. But it is inevitable that this becomes transparent because people will latch onto the smallest of details that don't impact the overall argument. In many cases, they seem to make up details to nitpick and doubt.

There is a rather famous case of triviality that demonstrates sowing seeds of doubt in action. A committee was appointed to design a nuclear power plant—a rather large undertaking, obviously. Yet the committee stalled for extended periods of time and was ultimately unable to complete the task because they could not agree on the design of a bike shed—literally a shed used to store bikes next to the reactor.

That was a true case of the inability to see the forest for the trees, and it's what people will do to you when they sow seeds of doubt. They will claim that your bike shed has problems and must be put up for debate, despite the fact that in the end, the bike shed doesn't impact the overall plan whatsoever.

People who sow seeds of doubt don't actually know or understand your argument. It's not about the argument or logic; it's just about winning a perceived competition. They just latch onto the first thing they can find a flaw with and hope that derails your overall argument.

For example, you propose a new public transport system that is based on trams, which are typically louder than normal buses. This person likely isn't aware of the statistical advantages in efficiency that trams offer over buses and metro systems or the fact that many countries in South America and Europe have employed similar systems to great success.

They don't care about all that. All they see is that you are proposing a system that they aren't interested in. That's all they need to know to go pick up and run with their argument. What's their argument?

But they'll be ugly. But they'll be so loud and disturb the peace. But...

In other words, this person doesn't really care about the practical reality of coming up with a solution. All this person is looking for is some sort of plausible or seemingly logical weakness in your proposition. They're just trying to poke holes and weaken your confidence.

If you suspect someone is trying to sow seeds of doubt to you, you just have to doubt their doubt. Call them out on it and ask them to be specific. Walk them through the thinking process of why you think a particular course of action makes more sense compared to others. Most importantly, ask why it matters in the grand scheme of your argument or proposal. Just as they innocently sowed seeds of doubt, you can also innocently ask their opinion here.

When you call them out as to why they doubt, they will be put on the defense. They'll have to justify their irrelevant argument and sound intelligent at the same time. There is no funnier sight that someone desperately trying to justify an argument that has zero basis while attempting to sound smart.

Since arguments are based on facts and logic can be applied to those facts, calling out their doubts and asking them to explain is a winning strategy. Nine times out of 10, these people are just going to draw a blank. Sowing the seeds of doubt is designed to simply trip you up.

Clarifying Questions

Sometimes you just come across people whose primary goal seems to be engaging and arguing with you. There's no rhyme or reason, as some people just get their buttons pushed by the sight of your face.

Whatever you say, they'll have a sarcastic retort for. There's no avoiding that they are going to try to pick your statements apart. When you encounter someone like this, your best defense is to overwhelm them with *clarifying questions*. When a person challenges something you say, they are almost always making an assertion. Assertions need to be based on something; otherwise, they are just opinions. But when someone makes an assertion, it is often put forth as a fact.

So if it's a fact, then where is the proof and backup for it? This is where your clarifying questions come into play. Since they are asserting something as a fact, they must bear the burden of proving themselves correct. Clarify exactly why they think they are correct and what evidence there is. Get them to clarify their position against your position.

What makes them think they are right and you are wrong?

Oh, can you tell me why it's wrong?
Where did you read that?
And what year was that study published?
Is that author actually legitimate?
So why do you think that contradicts what I

said?
What part exactly said it, and what did it say?
So why am I wrong?
Where is the flaw in my logic?

Done correctly, you essentially back the other person into a verbal corner and force them to admit their lack of knowledge.

Well, I don't really remember...
That's not my point...
Yeah, that's true too...

Many people adopt a smug look when they judge other people's positions. They throw all sorts of labels around, such as inaccurate, wrong, insane, exaggerated, or ignorant. They are well within their rights to do so. But you are within your rights to shift the burden of proof back to them with clarifying questions. Usually their smug look fades away quite quickly.

They claim that your proposition is wrong? Have them explain why they think it's wrong, in detail, with evidence. You're taking shots but you're not directly fighting back at your opponent. Best of all, if you phrase it innocently, you're just wondering about their stance.

Give them the task of rationalizing their objection so you can answer it point by point. This actually turns out beneficial for you, as you get chances to clarify your position further.

When people attack you without any justification or evidence, they are acting emotionally. People who are weak thinkers often speak with their emotions. They blurt out their discontent and unhappiness first, and logic follows if at all. They can't tell you their reasons. They just *feel* that way, and that doesn't help anyone.

Bring an element of logic, and use the opportunity to ask clarifying questions. Those who cannot back up their challenge will end up with egg on their face.

Beat the Strawman

This might be an argument tactic that you're familiar with or have possibly even used before.

The strawman argument finds flaws in arguments by oversimplifying it, taking it to the extreme, and attacking that version. That extreme version is the strawman, and it is so different from the actual argument that you don't even realize you are arguing against something that doesn't matter.

So it's actually not even attacking the actual argument put forth, just a disguised version that is superficially similar. It misrepresents the argument and inevitably makes it impossible. For instance:

John: I don't like birds that much.
Bob: So you're in favor of bird genocide? Where does it end? Mammal genocide?

The second person completely twisted the first person's words and misrepresented their position. That's the origin of the strawman—another opponent or argument is created, but they are illusory and thus made of straw. Fake. Conjured. Easily blown away.

Bob makes an argument that he can easily

refute and hopes that John doesn't quite notice the difference. The strawman puts words in the other person's mouth and ridicules those words. Fortunately for you, the strawman argument is usually relatively transparent and easy to defeat.

When you're not sure if you're faced with it, simply ask yourself the following question: what was the point I was making? Is the end conclusion actually what the alleged strawman is saying?

It's likely not, so you can call it out as manipulative, putting words in your mouth, and misrepresentation. More importantly, you can make it known that they are resorting to the strawman because they can't argue on your level. The strawman is frustrating because it is so commonplace. Just log onto Facebook and you'll see it in many forms.

Remember, someone has the sole purpose of making you look bad when they use it. They are purposefully lying and misrepresenting your position so that they can smash you down. They're not addressing the argument at that point; they are addressing you personally. Don't be afraid to take offense and call it out.

Takeaways:

- The time of self-defense has to end sometime, and sometimes the best defense is a good offense. Therefore, this chapter discusses some of the general methods to attack others, parry their attacks, and win arguments to get your way more often than not.
- There are many best practices for arguing and going on the offensive. Admittedly, some of them are about making the interaction less offensive overall. First, deal with the two separate problems of emotion and the situation. Second, use a three-step method of ask, validate, and join. Finally, avoid negative evaluations and focus on how you are affected by using "I feel" statements.
- Ad hominem is a sign of weakness where you argue against someone personally rather than their argument. Is emotional and illogical.
- Appeal to perfection is where you poke

one hole in an argument, and supposedly that is supposed to discredit everything. But that's a fallacy.
- Sowing seeds of doubt is where you poke holes in an argument but for the purpose of undermining their confidence in it.
- Clarifying questions is where you become a pedant and try to poke holes in other people's assertions and opinions.
- Beat the strawman is where you make sure to identify a strawman argument and diffuse it. Or you can create your own.

Conclusion

For many years, Kyle was such a big thorn in my side that I would get anxiety about going out sometimes. You can be prepared for war, but no matter how prepared, it doesn't mean you look forward to eventual clashes, especially of a personal nature.

But in many ways, learning to deal with someone like that was highly beneficial. We were forced into interaction with our friends, but that wasn't mandatory.

What if you faced a supervisor, coworker, or mother-in-law like this? How can you go about making them more than tolerable and actually rally them to your side as a friend?

More importantly, how can you diffuse

situations, defend yourself, and seize the respect that everyone deserves?

It's a lot of little things, and I hope I've taught you at least a few of them in this book.

I wouldn't say Kyle and I aren't the best of friends at this point in our lives, but that's not really the point or end goal. Previously, I was staring at a shut door every single day, and the door was made of titanium and adamantium. It wasn't something I could just force myself through.

Conversation tactics were the lockpicks I used to pry the door open and allow the possibility of friendship and connection. Sometimes that's all you can ask for, an opportunity, and that's not a bad thing! Even Tom Hanks, the most likable movie star in the world, has his detractors, and our best is all we can aspire to be.

Sincerely,

Patrick King
Social Interaction Specialist
www.PatrickKingConsulting.com

P.S. If you enjoyed this book, please don't be shy and drop me a line, leave a review, or both! I love reading feedback, and reviews are the lifeblood of Kindle books, so they are always welcome and greatly appreciated.

Speaking and Coaching

Imagine going far beyond the contents of this book and dramatically improving the way you interact with the world and the relationships you'll build.

Are you interested in contacting Patrick for:

- A social skills workshop for your workplace
- Speaking engagements on the power of conversation and charisma
- Personalized social skills and conversation coaching

Patrick speaks around the world to help people improve their lives as a result of the power of building relationships with improved social skills. He is a recognized industry expert, bestselling author, and speaker.

To invite Patrick to speak at your next event or to inquire about coaching, get in touch directly through his website's contact form at http://www.PatrickKingConsulting.com/contact, or contact him directly at Patrick@patrickkingconsulting.com.

Cheat Sheet

Chapter 1. Pre-Conversation

- Great conversations start before the actual conversation in the sense that there are many things you should do to prepare yourself to be charming and witty.
- You can get yourself ready for the interaction by warming up beforehand—psychologically and physically. Psychologically is a matter of getting in the mood to socialize and also becoming used to initiating interaction. This can be done with "10-second relationships," which plunge you into the deep end if

only for a moment. Physically, you should seek to warm up by reading out loud before socializing and making sure you exaggerate emotional expressiveness and variation. Read out loud three times and notice the difference in engagement, and you can instantly see the contrast of how you might come off.

- An additional way of preparing before conversations is to get your own information and life in order, and this can be done by following a conversation résumé. The purpose is to draw into your past and find what makes you an interesting person and make sure that is all at the tip of your tongue for easy usage.
- Fallback stories also have the same purpose. If you can create a fallback story, which has four simple components (bridge, story, your opinion, their opinion), you can walk into a conversation knowing that you can handle any awkward silence or topic change.

Chapter 2. Setting the Tone

- What determines whether you hit it off

with someone? It's not circumstantial; rather, it's a matter of you taking charge and setting the tone to be friendly and open. Most people treat others like strangers and thus won't become friends.
- The first way to set the tone then is to speak like friends: topic-wise, tone-wise, and even privacy-wise. People will go along with the tone you set as long as you aren't outright offensive. A powerful aspect of this is showing unfiltered emotion with people as friends do instead of filtering yourself and putting up a wall for the literal purpose of keeping people at a distance. Yes, this includes swearing and getting people to let their guards down.
- Another aspect of setting the right tone is to find and focus on similarities. When people observe similarity, they instantly open up and embrace it because it is a reflection of themselves. You can do this by creating similarities or digging for similarities.
- Finally, you can set the tone by getting people to talk even when they are closed off or seem intent on keeping you at an arm's length. You can do this by asking

specific questions that are irresistible for them to either comment on, explain, or defend—the questions aren't necessarily for them to actually answer.

Chapter 3. How to Be Captivating

- Captivating people usually refers to telling a story that leaves them listening like children. But there are many ways of creating this feeling in small, everyday ways. Storytelling is a big topic that is often made overly complex.
- An easy way to imagine everyday storytelling is that your life is a series of stories. Instead of giving one-word answers, get into the habit of framing your answers as a story with a point. It creates more engagement, lets you show your personality, and creates smoother conversation. The bonus here is that you can prepare these before a conversation.
- The 1:1:1 method of storytelling is to simplify it as much as possible. The impact of a story won't necessarily be stronger if it is 10 sentences versus two sentences. Therefore, the 1:1:1: method focuses on the discussion and reaction

that occurs after a story. A story can be composed solely of (1) one action, (2) one emotion to be evoked, and (3) a one-sentence summary.
- Telling stories is important, but what about eliciting them from others? You can phrase your questions carefully to ask for stories rather than answers from people, which is a simple way make conversation easier and more enjoyable for everyone involved.
- Stories can also be the basis for an inside joke. When you think about it, an inside joke is something that comes up multiple times with the same person and evokes a positive emotion. Thus, you just need to call back to a story through a conversation and there's a good chance it will stick as a "Remember when we talked about…" moment.

Chapter 4. Charm Offensive

- Whatever the reason, sometimes we find ourselves in a position where we *really* want to make a good impression. Normal conversation tactics to build rapport won't do here. What can really move the

needle?
- Obviously, the first way to charm people is to pay them compliments early and often. But there are specific compliments that really impact the recipients. You should seek to compliment people on things they have made a conscious choice about and that reflect their thinking process. This gives them validation in a way that complimenting them on their eyes simply doesn't.
- The charm offensive is powerful because it allows you to change people's perceptions of you. There is a process of converting an enemy to a friend, and it involves changing your own perception, invoking social proof, and creating or finding a common enemy.
- Finally, we've always learned that we shouldn't interrupt people. Normally, we shouldn't, but you have full permission to interrupt to agree and emphasize a shared emotion.

Chapter 5. Slipping Away and Out

- This may not be the most important skill overall, but it's the most important skill

for your sanity. How can we get away from people but in a graceful manner?
- There are many types of goodbyes and ways to leave. They are separate: leaving an event or party is not necessarily the same as leaving an interaction. As for leaving an event or party, the Irish Goodbye is particularly effective because it is actually a gesture of kindness for everyone involved. Otherwise, you can isolate your host, leave on a high note, or simply set expectations ahead of time so you feel less guilt about slipping away.
- Besides those, there are certain methods of getting away from interactions and people gracefully: the call, the bathroom, introductions, and using other people as pawns. These all share a few common elements to make these moves socially acceptable and subtle: having an excuse, creating urgency, asking for permission, and mentioning the future.

Chapter 6. Specific [Awkward] Situations

- Awkward situations occur just about every day, yet they are still awkward because we never learn how to deal with them. So how do you deal with awkward? By taking charge and setting the tone and eliminating the ambiguity that causes the awkward in the first place.

- But it's also helpful to provide blueprints on how to deal with common awkward situations you might come across. The first is forgetting someone else's name, and that's a matter of getting them to say their name without you directly asking. You can introduce them to someone else, ask for their contact info, ask them to spell their last name, or just fess up that you forgot and it's not personal.
- Accepting compliments is also something people handle with discomfort, and it's just a matter of deflecting the attention from yourself and complimenting the compliment. In this way, you can turn positivity one way into positivity for two people.
- Breaking the ice with strangers is never a comfortable feeling, but that's because it feels intrusive and rude. If you can give yourself a plausible reason for speaking to people, then you can easily interject and break the ice. For instance, you can ask for information or an opinion. You can

also comment on something that is shared or comment on something in the environment.
- Finally, dealing with interruptions can save your sanity because interruptions are frustrating. You can use a preemptive strike to let people know that you don't want to be interrupted. You can continually emphasize it and use it as a barometer to gauge who will respect your space. If you are the one who interrupts, then make it a habit to bring things back to what the other person was saying.

Chapter 7. Stop, Please

- You could be the most interesting person in the world and no one will care if you have annoying or repulsive conversational habits. Indeed, sometimes it is better to be more benign and less offensive.
- Annoying habit number one is to see things as only black and white, judge people, and try to control what they think. People will begin to avoid you.
- Annoying habit number two is to provide your unsolicited thoughts and advice to

people when they only want you to listen and validate them. Understand what people are seeking from you before answering or people will begin to avoid you.
- Annoying habit number three is creepy behaviors, which occur in both genders. Creepy behaviors have to do with making people uncomfortable with the amount of attention and focus they receive.
- Annoying habit number four is always laughing first instead of gauging people's reactions and letting them decide their humor for themselves. This is usually done out of insecurity and serves to impose your will on others.

Chapter 8. Self-Defense

- Dealing with people is not always easy because some of those people don't have the best of intentions toward you. In that case, it's important to understand how to defend yourself in conversation and keep your cool.
- One of the first ways to defend yourself is to defend your space and time. That's through learning how to gracefully say no

to people, places, and things. You can do this through your phrasing, creating categories, passing the buck, and creating hoops for people to jump through. These are all ways of avoiding a direct no that might offend someone.
- Deflecting insults and ridicule is also important to master. These are otherwise known as witty comebacks and make you part of the joke instead of the butt. The easiest ways to deflect insults are to use amplification or to redirect to something outlandish, both of which take the attention off you.
- Plan to admit you are wrong at least once during each argument or each occasion you are defending yourself. Your defense is more credible if you admit wrongdoing or fault, and it makes people lower their guards once they realize they're not going up against a brick wall.
- Passive-aggressive people are the worst. So here's a method for dealing with them. Don't give them what they want, don't get angry at them, speak their language of feeling wronged, give them clear incentives to act, and increase the cost for failure to comply.

Chapter 9. On the Offensive

- The time of self-defense has to end sometime, and sometimes the best defense is a good offense. Therefore, this chapter discusses some of the general methods to attack others, parry their attacks, and win arguments to get your way more often than not.
- There are many best practices for arguing and going on the offensive. Admittedly, some of them are about making the interaction less offensive overall. First, deal with the two separate problems of emotion and the situation. Second, use a three-step method of ask, validate, and join. Finally, avoid negative evaluations and focus on how you are affected by using "I feel" statements.
- Ad hominem is a sign of weakness where you argue against someone personally rather than their argument. Is emotional and illogical.
- Appeal to perfection is where you poke one hole in an argument, and supposedly that is supposed to discredit everything. But that's a fallacy.

- Sowing seeds of doubt is where you poke holes in an argument but for the purpose of undermining their confidence in it.
- Clarifying questions is where you become a pedant and try to poke holes in other people's assertions and opinions.
- Beat the strawman is where you make sure to identify a strawman argument and diffuse it. Or you can create your own.

Made in the USA
Lexington, KY
05 June 2018